COVENTRY LIBRARIES

Please return this book on or before
the last date stamped below.

/ 19

To renew this book take it to any of
the City Libraries before
the date due for return

Coventry City Council

FLYING FOR FREEDOM

ALOIS SISKA

Translated by
DAGMAR JOHNSON-SISKOVA

Pen & Sword
AVIATION

First published in Great Britain in 2008 by
PEN & SWORD AVIATION
an imprint of
Pen & Sword Books Ltd
47 Church Street, Barnsley, South Yorkshire, S70 2AS

ISBN 978-1-84415-730-3

The right of Alois Siska to be identified as the author of this work has been
asserted by him in accordance with the Copyright, Designs and Patents
Act 1988.

A CIP catalogue record for this book is
available from the British Library

Typeset by Concept, Huddersfield, West Yorkshire
Printed and bound in England by CPI UK

Pen & Sword Books Ltd incorporates the Imprints of
Pen & Sword Aviation, Pen & Sword Maritime, Pen & Sword Military,
Wharncliffe Local History, Pen & Sword Select,
Pen & Sword Military Classics and Leo Cooper

For a complete list of Pen & Sword titles please contact
PEN & SWORD BOOKS LIMITED
47 Church Street, Barnsley, South Yorkshire, S70 2AS, England
E-mail: enquiries@pen-and-sword.co.uk
Website: www.pen-and-sword.co.uk

To the crew of KX-B and 311 (Czechoslovak)
Squadron – our squadron.

Contents

Foreword ix
Translator's Introduction xi
Glossary xiii

Part 1
 1 Into the War 3

Part 2
 2 Direction South 23
 3 Escape from the Citadel 27
 4 Next Stop France 33
 5 311 Squadron 40
 6 Night Battle 45
 7 The Long Flights 49
 8 Third Year 56
 9 Wilhelmshaven 61
10 The Last Raid 67
11 Shipwrecked 72
12 Lost Hope 78
13 Happy New Year, 1942 85
14 We Fight Death 91
15 Windmills 95
16 Terra Firma 98
17 Prisoners of War 105
18 Sagan 112
19 Arrest 118
20 The Gestapo Move In 124

21 Whatever Next? 131
22 Days of Freedom 138

Part 3
23 Until the Bitter End 147

Epilogue 175

Foreword

It is indeed a privilege to provide a tribute to my old friend Czech Guinea Pig Alois Siska, a man whose bravery has my fullest admiration and respect.

Our flying experiences during the 1939–45 War were similar; we both flew in Wellington bombers and were both badly injured. We were also patients at the Queen Victoria Hospital, East Grinstead, Sussex, England and we shared the same brilliant innovative plastic surgeon, the late Sir Archibald McIndoe. Both of us also became members of the world-famous organization, the Guinea Pig Club.

I was more fortunate than Alois in other respects. My crippled aircraft was at least able to reach the sanctuary of England where I crashed. I was treated with kindness, consideration and understanding, while he had the misfortune to crash into the North Sea. One member of his crew died in the aircraft, while he with four others clambered aboard a rubber dinghy and drifted for six days. During this nightmare two crew members died from frostbite, thirst and hunger, and Alois also had to endure the injuries he received when the aircraft plunged into the sea.

On the sixth day they sighted land and were able to paddle the dinghy ashore, but their euphoria ended and turned to despair when they realized they had arrived in Holland, which was occupied by the Germans.

After four horrible years in captivity Alois was finally freed by the American forces in 1945, and was eventually sent to East Grinstead for medical treatment that he had been denied as a prisoner of war.

He returned to Prague in 1947 only to find the incumbent government disapproved of his escape from occupied Czechoslovakia to fight in the Royal Air Force, and once again he had to endure all kinds of humiliation.

Alois was a remarkable person who, in spite of the privations, managed to rise above it all and maintain his courage and pride. For me the highlight of the Guinea Pig Club's reunions was the moment when Alois Siska arrived – we would welcome each other with warmth that only brothers can achieve.

Jack J. Toper MBE
Chairman and Editor of the Guinea Pig Club

Translator's Introduction

My father started writing this book while recovering from his war wounds in the Queen Victoria Hospital in East Grinstead immediately after the Second World War. He returned to Czechoslovakia just in time for the communist takeover of February 1948, one outcome of which was government censure of all Czechs who had fought the Nazis from the West, mainly ex-members of the RAF. His initial manuscript consequently stayed hidden until the early 1960s, when a temporary political thaw allowed such a story to be published.

The first publication was a labour of love by the entire family. I still remember my mother typing the pages on Grandpa's old portable typewriter. The result, the first edition, was a modest paperback which arrived in the bookshops of Prague in July 1966 and sold out within days; a hardback edition in Slovak was published the following year. But after the fraternal help of the Soviet bloc armed forces in 1968 and the subsequent return of a hardline government, the book had to be shelved again. It did not reappear until after the Velvet Revolution of 1989, when ex-members of the RAF were finally rehabilitated and shown the respect they so richly deserved. The book was extended to include the post-1948 era to complete the story.

My father originally wrote his story for his own countrymen. For a British readership a direct translation would have represented certain difficulties, so he glossed over some specifically Czech anecdotes, as they would be common knowledge to all Czechs but nonsensical to a British reader. And my father has explained at length certain war stories – such as Douglas Bader and his presence in Colditz – with which most Britons are familiar, but would be unknown to Czechs. With that in mind, and with my husband's help, I have adapted these passages in the book to make sense to all.

For me, as a translator, this is the end of a very long road. My father's story, and that of other members of his squadron, has been part of my growing up. And for Mum and me, 311 Squadron became *our* squadron – cherished, respected and held in awe. It was my father's dream to have his book published in England, the country which became his second home. We agreed but sadly Dad died before this translation could be completed.

Dagmar Johnson-Siskova

Glossary

Part 1

Sokol – Czech physical education organization established in 1862 by Tyrs & Fugner to promote physical and spiritual well-being amongst the mass of the population.

Part 2

Gooseneck – Part of the flare path along a runway.

POW – Prisoner of War.

'Roll out the Barrel' – This is actually an English version of the chorus of the Czech song 'Skoda Lasky', composed by Jaromir Vejvoda in 1910.

SBO – Senior British Officer.

The Good Soldier Svejk – A novel about an incompetent Czech soldier before the First World War, written by Josef Chapka.

Part 3

CPK – Flight Simulator.

CSPB – Czechoslovak Union of Anti-Fascist Fighters was a civil organization formed in 1948 by joining together various resistance units from both the First and Second World Wars.

ICAO – International Civil Aviation Organization.

JZD – Co-operative Farm.

LNP 1 – 1st Auxiliary Air Force Group.

LNP 2 – 2nd Auxiliary Air Force Group (stationed in the town of Ceske Budejovice in southern Bohemia).

LVA – Air Force Academy (military).

MNO – Ministry of Defence.

MNV – Parish Council.

Narodni Fronta – Formed in Moscow in 1945 whose main purpose was 'to unify and coordinate general political awareness of all citizens in accordance with the programme of the Communist Party'.

OBZ – Military Intelligence renamed the Fifth Department after the coup of 1948. Used the nature of their work as a cover for political purges against anybody the new regime disapproved.

ONV – District Council.

OVS – District Military Council. Dealt with all military personnel matters on a district level.

SDL – Civil Aviation Authority.

SNV – Night Vision School.

TPZS – Technical Fire & Rescue Service.

ULZ – Institute of Aviation Medicine.

PART ONE

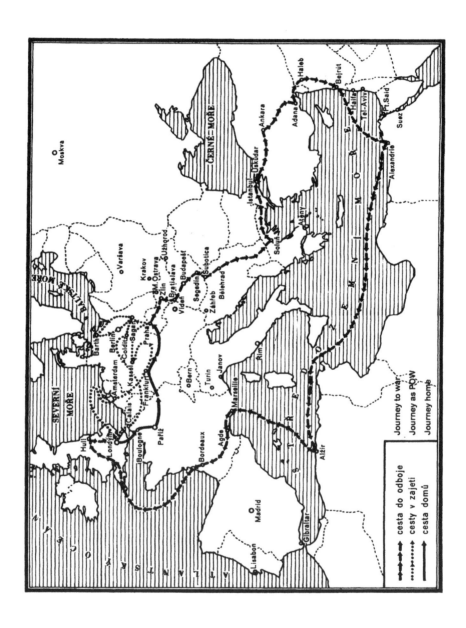

SEVERNÍ MOŘE

ČERNÉ MOŘE

BALTSKÉ MOŘE

ATLANTSKÝ OCEÁN

STŘEDOZEMNÍ MOŘE

Moskva

Varšava

Krakov

Uzhgorod

M.Ostrava

Zlín

Bratislava

Budapešť

Vídeň

Segedín

Subotica

Záhřeb

Bělehrad

Berlín

Colditz

Kassel

Sagan

Praha

Frankfurt

Amsterdam

Bern

Turín

Bartin

Hull

Londýn

Calais

Boulogne

Paříž

Bordeaux

Agde

Marseille

Rím

Janov

Madrid

Lisabon

Gibraltar

Alžír

Istanbul

Üsküdar

Ankara

Adana

Haleb

Bejrút

Haifa

Tel-Aviv

Pt.Said

Suez

Alexandrie

Atény

Soluň

Journey to war

Journey as POW

Journey home

cesta do odboje

cesty v zajetí

cesta domů

Chapter 1

Into the War

I was born in a little village called Lutopecny near the town of Kromeriz. We had a smallholding and I had two older siblings. My brother was already working and my sister was still at home.

Once, in my pre-school years, I was helping my mother in the fields. We were hoeing swedes when I heard the noise of an aircraft engine. I stopped working and gazed at that magnificent flying machine in the cloudless sky. I followed its progress until it disappeared, ignoring my mother's demand to concentrate on the work in hand. My desire to fly was untameable.

My father died in the First World War on 18 November 1914 on the Russian front. I was born on 15 May that year. Many years later, when I came home after the war, my mother and I visited some relative in the town of Kojetin. While browsing through the family photographs, including some of my father, my cousin suddenly remembered: 'You know what? When you were about four, you claimed that you would build an aeroplane and fly to Russia to find your father.'

My desire to fly grew stronger with time. While an apprentice, I made my first model aircraft – radial engines out of tin, little struts holding the wings ... I should perhaps add that until then I had never seen a stationary plane either on the ground or in a photograph.

Later, at Prostejov flying school, I showed my first model to Staff Sergeant Ruprecht who immediately said, 'That's Boska.' When I explained to him how I made it, he could hardly believe it.

I have an admission to make. Since my school days I had always been scathing about anybody who failed to comply with rules and regulations, and who did not fulfil their promises. It certainly got me into trouble many times in later life, but it also gained me respect. I preferred that.

While attending my school in Kromeriz, my class teacher Miss Kourilova always had some good advice to offer. She also gave me a Czech translation of the book by O. Swet Marden, *Whatever you do, do it well*. This became my private bible. After school I trained to be a mechanic.

I was over eighteen when I first applied to join the flying school in Prostejov, only to be told that they did not take on anybody over eighteen.

I had one last chance. I knew that in Otrokovice, Bata had his own flight – after all I had wandered nearby many a time, just to get nearer the planes, even to the extent of taking my chances and travelling without a ticket, as by then I had joined the ranks of the unemployed and did not have much money. It was the 1930s and the economic crisis was acutely felt by many. But what wouldn't I have done for my dream!

During these short visits I watched the French aircraft mechanics working, their obligatory cigarette hanging from the corner of their mouths. There was very little one could pick up through the half-open hangar doors, but the atmosphere was good enough for me ... just to be close.

I also knew that the flight employed wireless operators who qualified through Bata's work experience scheme. I tried to join that, but the answer was the same as from the flying school. However, it also said that I could get in through joining the construction group building the railway from Vizovice to the Slovak town of Puchov – over the Vizovice hills. It was basically a working opportunity for the scores of unemployed, qualified workers who had lost their jobs in the crisis.

I joined in November 1932. That winter I found myself in a situation which opened the door for me.

With a friend we were working at the entrance to the next tunnel. He was digging and I was hammering together the lagging. Close by was a small gorge full of water, with the pylons of the new railway bridge sticking out. I felt a sudden tremor. Oh no! I did not think twice and pulled my friend down into the water with me. The entrance to the tunnel filled up behind us.

They pulled us out, soaked and freezing. We changed into dry clothes and had a hot toddy. It could have been the end for us.

The boss of the company we were working for was Mr Klinovsky, who also ran a local Sokol group in Vizovice. He congratulated me for my effort in front of the whole company and as a reward suggested an apprenticeship at Bata's engineering college in Zlin. That I accepted, goes without saying.

The apprenticeship came with accommodation and we had to clock in every morning at seven sharp. Theory and practical training went hand in hand. During the morning we gradually learned our way around the factory floor and its plant, and there were lessons in the afternoon.

In 1934, Mr Bata gained a licence to build light aircraft. I was chosen to join his new company, Zlin Aircraft Works Ltd., which was based at Otrokovice airfield. I was amongst those working on the prototype of the famous Zlin Z-XII. As a reward for an invention, I chose pilot training instead of money. My dream had come true. I passed the test and gained my pilot's licence. I will never forget that day – 29 September 1936.

During the late 1930s, with the sabre rattling of our western neighbour already being heard, I began my national service, together with another forty recruits.

Nothing strange about that as it happened to many young men every year. The difference was that amongst scores of new recruits, forty of us already had a pilot's licence. We were expected to improve our flying skills as first participants of the new scheme 'Thousand Pilots for the Republic' – in the current political situation, a very sensible idea indeed.

As we knew the basics already, we were to receive full, albeit shortened, military flying training – the same syllabus as attendees of the Flying School in Prostejov, but in half the time. The only difference was that we received our airman's pay from the start, unlike the regular attendees who were not eligible until the beginning of their practical flying – after the first year.

They split us into two identical groups. One started the day with flying practice and the other in the classroom; we swapped after lunch. The lessons were not too bad, although there was a lot to learn. But the practical flying proved trickier. We were well aware of the difference between civilian and military training, so were not under any illusions, but the reality surpassed any novice's expectations. Our training so far proved to be elementary indeed, in the true sense of the word. We knew how to take off and land, hold the course and horizon, complete some easy manoeuvres, and some of us could perform a short landing on the wing. But the E-39 we had to handle now was a different kettle of fish altogether. Even during the first flight we faced forty-five minutes of sharp turns, spins and rolls on full throttle and without. When this was over, I could hardly locate my own airfield, even though it was only a few miles from the training air space.

My situation was probably not helped by being called every farm animal there was in a constant stream belting out of the one-way intercom. I could not see any of them on the ground below and eventually realized the instructor was talking to me.

For a while after the landing my balance was out of synch. It took a while to grasp that what I was standing on was the ground, the hangars were not flying and the sky was in the right place. Some were much worse off.

If I had not wanted to become a military pilot so badly I would probably have given up there and then, but by then I had already finished the Pilot Officer course with the 1st Air Force Group based in Cheb. My next stop was the Military Flying School in Prostejov. Only after that did I join Olomouc Group.

While in Prostejov I realized more than ever that I had to forget my civilian past. Until then I naively believed that if somebody at the age of twenty-two was already qualified in his job, had a driving licence, basic pilot's licence and attended the gym twice a week, they would survive in the military. I was wrong!

During my first week my instructor told me abruptly, 'You're not in the gym anymore, this is military … I'm not interested in your civilian experience. Three times round the courtyard – now, and get a move on!'

By the time I finished the third lap round the courtyard of Stefanik Barracks, I regretted that I had not sent home, amongst other things, my civilian persona.

When, breathing heavily, I reported back, my instructor acknowledged my salute and barked, 'Turn round, stand still, left turn, stand at ease! You see, you can do it!'

Not surprisingly, our meagre flying experience was not well received. They took advantage of it and reported back that the whole experiment had failed, and had to be stopped immediately. The reply came straight back: 'You are the instructors, it's your job to teach them!' They put us through our paces after that, but it made their lives hard too.

Our instructor was a certain Staff Sergeant Ruprecht, a short stocky man. Once, at dawn, while helping the mechanics to prepare our training E-39s, he was busying himself behind the controls of an Avia B-534. Our first E-39 already sat on the strip, ready for take-off, when the sound of the B-534's engines stopped. After a while one of the other instructors muttered, 'Watch it, Ruprecht is crawling in.' We all lifted our heads but could not see any plane over the airfield. Suddenly the uneven rumble of the engines came from the direction of the landing zone and the plane popped out of the morning mist just above the ground. Right at the end of the strip the sound died down and the plane landed. The engine picked up again and with the tail up the plane taxied towards the hangar.

He knew how to land as a fighter pilot and just wanted to show off his special manoeuvre, which later was my undoing. Just before we were allowed on our first solo flight, I had a disagreement with him and as a punishment he forbade me – the only one from our group – to take part and left for the canteen.

I was deeply disappointed. It was almost noon and most of our group had completed their solo flights. I was sitting with three other friends nearby, watching the others landing and reporting back to the testing instructor, Flying Officer Seidl. I could barely hold back the tears. His second in command, Pilot Officer Domansky, listed all the names. Flying Officer Seidl asked the inevitable question, 'Who's not been out there yet?'

I stood to attention and reported that it was me.

'Why not?'

'I was told I am not good enough.'

'How come? I heard that you were so good that you were being set up as an example.'

I shrugged my shoulders, head bowed.

'Test him,' he ordered Domansky.

We put on our parachutes, picked up the helmets and goggles and went off. The mechanic started the engine, the instructor did the checks and said, 'She's yours. Let's roll.'

I taxied towards the edge of the strip and as soon as I took up the position, I heard, 'Take off!'

I took off at the designated 'T' landing mark, climbed to 300 metres, performed four correct turns and headed back down. During the last turn I closed the throttle and started gliding towards the airfield. It felt as if I was on my own as the instructor had not said a word.

There was no wind and I did not want to overshoot. No training plane had any brakes and if you overshot the 'T', you failed. I was expecting some comment from the back. As soon as we stopped, I heard, 'That was really good! Let's do it once more. Get on with it!'

My second flight was about the same, only this time 10 metres before the 'T'. Comments from the back were to the point, 'Flipping hell, good again. Right, third time lucky, as they say!'

I was less nervous by now but concentrated hard not to make a mistake. As I was descending towards the edge, I spotted Staff Sergeant Ruprecht returning from the canteen. I executed the required three-point landing and to my – and perhaps also instructor's surprise – the plane stopped dead on the 'T'.

'That was good, switch off and report landing!' came from the back. While I was reporting my landing, I heard the Staff Sergeant.

'Did you see it, idiots? That was some landing. Who landed it? And where is Siska?'

Before my colleagues could say anything, I stood in front of him and reported my landing. Silence followed. He kept looking at us, but the Flying Officer stepped in.

'You can praise Siska, he deserves it. He landed well and can easily go solo.'

Perhaps out of absent-mindedness, perhaps on purpose, he did not acknowledge my report or congratulate me. He merely barked, 'Turn round! Bend forward!'

A gentle kick up my posterior made everybody laugh.

Next day we all continued flying solo well into the fading light.

'No more take-offs, that's enough for today. Who is still up?'

'Last one to land, Sir. But the wind has changed direction; we should adjust the "T".'

'Who is up there and how good is he?' inquired the Flying Officer.

My instructor confirmed it was his trainee and that he was doing well.

'Let's go for it then. Hopefully he'll manage.'

By then we were all standing around and watched the approaching plane. The course was good, but he had to overcome the side wind. He was partially gliding and because he was too short, he had to use the throttle. When he missed the edge of the strip, our anxiety grew.

'Send him back up!' one of the other instructors yelled.

'No, that might be worse … and it's getting late,' the Flying Officer retorted and added, 'hopefully he'll get it this time.'

As far as the trainee was concerned, his main task was to land in the direction of the 'T'. Lack of experience, maybe also fear of making his own decision, resulted in him landing in the direction he was in. As soon as the wheel touched the ground, the wing tip clipped it too and the whole plane tipped forward. It all happened so quickly that the subsequent full flip felt like watching a slow-motion film. By the time we reached the plane, the trainee was hanging out of the cockpit, head first. We got him out, unhurt but badly shaken, and he proceeded to report his landing. Nobody criticized him. They all knew the main reason was not his lack of knowledge.

The days grew longer at the beginning of April, spring was in the air and our training programme with the E-39 was almost at an end. Our last prescribed manoeuvre was an emergency landing with the engine switched off from a height of 700 metres. After two years with an instructor I was finally allowed to perform this solo. The landing was good, the plane came to a standstill just before the 'T' and for me it was all over.

I watched others in the warm sun with a measurable degree of satisfaction. Those of us who had finished for the day were sun-bathing. It was quite an atmosphere. In silence we watched another well-executed solo landing. The Station Commander asked, 'Any-one else for a solo?'

The last trainee explained that his instructor would not let him go solo. As before, the Station Commander appointed Warrant Officer First to take him up. Everybody was watching. We had the feeling something was amiss when the climb up to 700 metres took longer than usual and with growing concern we watched the plane per-forming a short circuit at the far end of the airfield. Even from a distance we could see the instructor rising from his back seat as if he wanted to lean over the trainee's head. The next minute the plane nose-dived and the instructor fell out, his parachute opened and he safely headed for the ground. Nobody worried about him any more as our attention was fully focused on the unfortunate trainee pilot.

'I do hope he doesn't cut the engine now.' The Station Commander expressed everybody's thought.

But his wish was granted and after another circuit the plane landed. The ambulance in the meantime collected Warrant Officer First, walking back with his parachute under his arm.

The reason for this escapade?

The test instructor had repeatedly ordered a climb to 700 metres, but used the intercom for verbal messages, so the trainee could only acknowledge by nodding his head. The Warrant Officer always wanted to double-check the instrument panel to make sure his order had been carried out correctly, so he unclipped his seat harness in order to see the instrument panel, and as soon as the poor trainee felt his presence behind, he ducked. The outcome was inevitable, the plane nose-dived and the instructor was catapulted out. An incorrectly set-up altimeter could cause a serious accident, but luckily it all ended well. The instructor was called before the Commanding Officer and reprimanded.

The next stage of our training was on – for us – a completely new plane, the Praga E-41. The E-41 was powered by an in-line, glycol-cooled engine and the radiators had a habit of cracking if overheated, which would mean an emergency landing.

We started with dual controls as before and followed the obligatory sequence of manoeuvres. What was new this time was mapping our own flight paths, and single and double descending spins. The latter were practised to perfection. The former were solo, high-altitude, orienteering flights at 3,000 metres along the railway line Prostejov–Kromeriz–Prerov–Prostejov with an estimated flight time of thirty-five minutes. Those who went out first had nothing to fear, but the overheating got worse later as the air warmed up and for that reason nobody was allowed to take off after 1100 hrs.

One day a plane was delayed. Before the rest of us finished for the morning, it was obvious that he must have landed somewhere else. The question was, where and how well? Before we adjourned for lunch, we received a short message from the police station in Kromeriz: 'Emergency landing of an E-41 near the village of Selesovice. Pilot unhurt.'

When the Commanding Officer told us, I volunteered to go with the mechanics to collect the plane as I came from that area and an unscheduled trip was welcome. Even before we got to the village, we spotted the white plane in the middle of a field of clover. The local bobby was desperately trying to keep the inquisitive villagers away from it.

While the mechanics were getting the plane ready for transportation, their boss and I went into the village to collect the pilot. I found him in the mayor's house at a table laden with a lot of tasty food. As far as the mayor was concerned, this was a special occasion and he felt it his duty to provide the appropriate refreshments. As far as our poor pilot was concerned, he was about to be saved. It was during the harvest time and it was hot. Although the mayor's two daughters were suitably dressed for the weather, our poor chap was wearing a fully lined flying suit with nothing but a pair of pants underneath, so he could not take it off. The sweat was pouring down his reddened face. Not surprisingly, he was not enjoying the food ... but the rest of us did.

An important part of our training was also basic military foot drill, which also meant regular sentry duties. As every effort was made for us not to miss out on any lessons or practical training, we took over guard duties during weekends.

There were two peculiarities. First was the actual ritual of changing of the guard. Amongst the officers was one who revelled in this routine duty, especially if it was raining. Then it would take up to two hours before the guard change was completed. At the start of our duty we always had to present our full kit and all hell broke loose if he found a single missing pencil or card. On discovering such a serious breach of regulations, we were sent back and another line-up was called twenty minutes later. For him and us it meant shorter duty but the previous guard would not be well pleased. When we eventually arrived at the sentry box soaked to the skin and covered in mud, we would be met by a barrage of abuse for being so stupid.

Another unpleasant side was night duty at the damaged No. 3 Hangar. During windy or stormy nights one could hear nothing else for the noise of the broken corrugated-iron panels, not even the new sentry coming in. We had no chance of spotting the inspecting officer or an intruder.

11

I cannot remember anybody looking forward to this duty as we all remembered too well the fate of one of the pilots who were practising for the world air championship in Zurich. This involved a time-limited climb to 3,000 metres, followed by a nosedive on full throttle, and pull-out at 500 to 250 metres above ground. One of the contenders for this particular discipline was Warrant Officer Pacak.

To avoid us he usually started his practice with an Avia B-534 at dawn. One morning, while in the nosedive with the engine roaring, a wing broke off and the uncontrollable plane, with the pilot trapped inside it, hit the hangar full of planes. The hangar exploded and all the planes inside were either completely destroyed or badly damaged. The engine and the pilot disappeared under the concrete floor. All that was left from the wings and the fuselage were a few splinters, amongst them Pacak's left wrist and his watch. He probably tried to get out but ran out of time. His tragic death marred an otherwise successful third, fourth and fifth places achieved by our airmen in Zurich.

After completing our basic military pilot's training we started combat flying on an Aero Ap-32 on 1 June. Even their appearance – dark green as opposed to the training silver – exuded their combat role and the massive nine-cylinder aerial Jupiter engines with 450 hp suggested a different type of flying altogether.

After the initiation flight we started learning spins, turns and, for the first time, the sideslip. I particularly liked this one, mainly because the plane so willingly went into the manoeuvre and so easily came out of it again. Another reason was that my instructor and I saw eye to eye from the start. I therefore assumed that our previous disagreement during basic training was well and truly forgotten, but I was mistaken ...

We were returning from a longish combat training flight and were above the barracks at 350 metres with only a field of corn between the landing strip and us. In my mind I was already preparing for my favourite short landing when the instructor's voice came through, 'What are you going to do about your height?'

Not only did I know what to do, but I did not actually have any choice. So I kept nodding vigorously and carried on. A mere few seconds before I intended to bring the plane into the sideslip, the familiar farm-animal address deafened me and I simultaneously felt the sudden change of our rudders. We entered the sideslip. As I always fully respected the rule that the overall control of the plane belongs to the instructor, I took my hands off the controls and re-sentfully accepted that I would not land the plane myself. The plane was dropping fast but I was not worried – not until the point where I would have levelled the plane as we were still some distance from the edge of the strip and one of our wings was nearing the cornfield too fast. In the next moment – after another scream through the intercom – the plane levelled and the engine roared, but it was too late for it to make up for the loss of speed.

Our undercarriage clipped the track between the field and the airstrip, and after three jumps we landed. The instructor taxied quickly towards the hangar. Before the propeller stopped and I managed to unclip myself, he pulled me out of the cockpit and threw me on the ground. He yelled that we could both have been killed – it turned out that at the time of the sideslip neither of us was actually flying the plane. Fortunately we got away with it and not long after, during another charged situation, we became good friends.

Once we had finished our practical training and passed the un-avoidable exams, our stay in Prostejov was over.

They woke us up at three in the morning. The small courtyard of Vyskov Castle was shrouded in darkness – a typical raw September morning. The Duty Sergeant had to hold the paraffin lamp over the list of pilots and observers of our squadron so the Squadron Leader could call out our names. Nobody was absent.

He had to pause so the armourer could issue each of us with a pistol and two rounds. The situation was serious.

The mechanics were busy warming up the last few planes; it was still twilight. While we were putting on our full flying kit, they brought us fresh coffee. The Squadron Leader appointed the crews and allocated the planes. I was given a brand-new S-328 plane with a radio.

Our destination was the advanced airfield north-east of the town of Ivanovice Na Hane, which was not far.

'Take off in threes, height 200 metres, landing individually,' was our order.

I was on the right wing of the first flight, lead by Sergeant Cyrda Sebela. The engine was humming happily and the plane smelt of new paint. It was lighter higher up and Cyrda gave the order to move in. As we approached Ivanovice he gave the order to disperse for landing. Below us, against the dark background was the 'T' and on our left, with identification lights on, another flight.

The airfield sloped slightly but we all landed well, covered the planes with branches and went to get our orders. All punishments were cancelled. My twenty-one days of solitary confinement for disobeying orders during target practice – flying too low over the target – would start on our return to barracks.

The first lorries with supplies arrived, followed by some locals, both old and young, bringing refreshments. We pilots – and I was a corporal by then – were billeted in town. By that evening we felt as if we had lived there all our lives. My observer and I were put up with the family of the local brickmaker, whose hospitality was endless. We had to take their only bedroom; no argument was allowed. We could smell coffee and freshly baked cakes from the kitchen.

On the night of mobilization, the radio was playing the signature tune regularly interspersed by the message: 'Special announcement to follow...'

It was well after ten. A small child slept peacefully in his father's arms; the old woman's hands rested on her lap; the brickmaker slowly filled his pipe; the young mother sat staring into the corner. Nobody spoke. The repetitive signature tune was getting on everybody's nerves as a little wooden dove suspended from the ceiling gently turned in the warm air of the room. The old clock on the wall had stopped at 2200 hrs and the wall calendar read 23 September 1938.

'Attention – attention ... The President will address the nation ...'
We all froze.
Mobilization!
'All reservists report to their units.'
'We have to go,' said both father and son. The mother picked up the child as the old woman wiped away her tears. As the men got ready, a few cakes were packed for the journey. Then a short goodbye ... they were in a hurry.

The following morning, when it was still dark, the whole squadron was addressed by the Squadron Leader. We had to be ready for an immediate take-off at dawn. Additional arms were issued: four machine guns and six small bombs.

'The mission won't be easy and there will be casualties. Any volunteers?' the Squadron Leader asked.

We all raised our hands and he looked at us for a moment, lost for words. There were more crews than planes. The chosen ones were considered lucky.

But the order never came. The Munich Agreement turned all our hopes and resolutions into bitterness and humiliation.

Several months later, on that fateful March day, the sky leaden with wet snow, the boots of the occupying forces trampled on our last hopes. We learned that day in our squadron that no appeasement with the enemy would secure peace. We were demobbed and lost everything. We airmen lost our planes and our arms, students lost their schools and universities, and every citizen his freedom. Only the burning desire for revenge grew stronger with every day. We were looking for opportunities to fight.

The first illegal escapes across the border weren't aimed either to the east or to the west, but north, to Poland. Not everybody succeeded, the Gestapo were everywhere and willing informers also helped. Those who failed faced the concentration camp, but it did not deter further attempts. When Poland fell, we started looking for other options. France was our only hope.

The occupation brought many changes and all activity on our airfield stopped. The Germans took over our canteen and installed a machine gun on its roof. In the Zlin factory, all flying personnel were assigned to various jobs in Bata's aircraft factory, mainly on transport planes. Two Germans at the entrance gate checked all of us thoroughly every morning. German so-called technical supervisors took their place on the factory floor, poking their noses into everything and everywhere.

The natural reaction of the workers was an instant resistance towards the occupiers and they hid anything which could possibly assist the Germans in their expansion plans. One of those was a prototype aircraft called the Zlin Z-XIII. A rather elegant low-wing monoplane, powered by a Walter Major Mk 4 engine, this aircraft was one of the first fitted with wing flaps and a variable-pitch propeller. Before the occupying force could spot it, its appearance was altered and it was hidden in the far corner of the workshop, waiting

15

for better times to come. So far so good. They had not found it yet, though it was only a matter of time. The number of arrests by the Gestapo was growing.

It was necessary to form illegal resistance groups and, through those, co-ordinate any clandestine activity and organize further escapes – first via Poland, later via the Slovak State, Hungary, Yugoslavia, the Balkans, Syria and by ship to France.

I became involved from the start. Once during the factory holiday I escorted one escapee to the town of Moravska Ostrava, but I was late back. Despite a hurriedly arranged emergency visit to my sick mother and a temporary cooling-off period of my illegal activities, I could not avoid suspicion. Soon afterwards my boss Eman Krejci appeared by my lathe with some drawings, the safest way to ask me to come and see him at home later. He did not say anything else. I could hardly wait until the end of my shift, knowing something was up, as Eman was the leader of our resistance group.

As soon as his wife brought us coffee and took up her watch by the window, Eman broached the subject: 'The Germans are getting interested in the Z-XIII. We have to get it out of the country to Yugoslavia.'

I took a deep breath and tried to guess what my role could be in this daring plan. Eman continued, 'We have to expect German counter-activity, so you are the obvious choice. You're single, don't live at home and most of all you can gain legitimate access to the plane. Others would cause suspicion if they tried to enter the work-shop. Because of your slight built you also are best suited for a long-distance flight. We have every confidence in you. But the final decision is yours, of course.'

I cannot remember how much time passed and what thoughts entered my head before Eman took another sip of coffee and asked, 'Will you do it?'

I nodded.

After that Eman explained the plan.

I was given more detailed instructions on the plane during the afternoon shifts which were not so busy, so it was easier to escape any unwanted German attention. Eman was best qualified for this as he was the mechanic who accompanied Major Ambrus and the plane to France in 1937.

Eman wasn't the talkative type, but what he had to say, was worth listening to.

'The propeller will have the optimum adjustment, which is good especially at take-off as we have to replace the battery with a reserve tank.'

He proceeded to explain to workings of the flaps, specified the take-off speed and took me through the instrument panel. All I had to do was remember it all, memorize the cockpit drill and keep my mouth shut.

During the next few weeks I took every opportunity to go through the routine, at the same time getting used to the shape of the long, high-sided cockpit. When I was on morning shifts I pretended to be sick and spent my time studying the route.

Although I had finished my military air force training some months earlier, I willingly accepted Eman's advice, and also from the senior pilot, Mr Ourednicek.

I split the entire route to Yugoslavia into separate sections and marked the correct courses and any useful landmarks. After I had memorized everything, I practised take-off and landing with my eyes shut. The longer all this took, the more restless I became at work and got reprimanded several times. It was beginning to play on my nerves.

Eventually one Saturday Eman approached me in the usual manner. While he busied himself with spreading the drawing in front of me, he muttered, 'Sunday night at eight at my place. Make sure nobody sees you!'

He showed me some details of the part in question and left before the German guard could get any nearer. I did not do a great deal after that.

On the Saturday night, in order to avoid the nagging thoughts, I spent the evening in the café of our local Municipal House, and went out for dinner on the Sunday night before seeing Eman. Could it be my last in my occupied homeland?

I headed for Eman's house along the footpath at the edge of the airfield to avoid being spotted, stopping several times to gaze at the airfield where I had started my flying on the Z-XII well before becoming a military pilot. I arrived at Eman's on time and after a few general queries he broached the subject.

'Apart from your faked illness I presume you are OK?' I could confirm that. Eman carried on, 'Tomorrow morning you will not go to work at six, but you have to be at the back of the workshop hangar by five. It will be open and the mechanics will be preparing a Z-XII for test flying. The Germans have agreed to it. But be very careful! Lada Svab will take off with the first "twelve" and while they warm up other planes, your "thirteen" will be warming up at the back. You will get in and as soon as Lada gets outside the airspace above the airfield, you'll take off! The Germans should not spot this as you will turn sharp left and disappear behind the hill just as Lada will appear again. Keep her low during take-off. You will need to gain enough speed to execute the sharp turn safely. Keep her low and at 300 kph until you reach Hungary. They shouldn't be able to fire at you. By the time their supervisors arrive just before six, you should be well on your way.'

His instructions were so positive that I could already see myself in the cockpit. When he finished, my mind was racing. I tried to find the words to express my feelings – that I would not fail, or words to that effect – but failed completely. Eman picked up the newspaper and handed over a pistol and one cartridge.

'This is just in case. You shouldn't need it, but it's safer that way.'

It was clear outside. We said our goodbyes and I disappeared into the darkness, covering those first few yards from Eman's house to the railway crossing with my mind completely blank.

Only the sound of the approaching feet brought me back to reality. I must not be seen!

I felt that anybody could see what I was about to do. I crossed to the other side of the road, facing the ditch as any tired pub-crawler would. Somebody walked past ... nothing happened. I continued past my flat towards Napajedla as far as the exact spot from which I would approach the hangar. I knew every inch, every bush – it was after all the view from my bedroom window. After I'd checked the route a few more times, I headed home.

The house was quiet. As I pulled the pistol out of my pocket and pushed in the cartridge I could still hear Eman's voice: 'You shouldn't need it, but it's safer that way!'

I remembered the time of mobilization in 1938 when I was also given a pistol. It was bigger and came with two cartridges. I did not use it then ... My main task now was the flight out. I had to concentrate on that.

I put the pistol in the pocket of my leather overcoat, prepared my clothing for the journey and checked everything I was leaving behind, to avoid endangering anybody I knew. I picked up my little book by O. Swett Marden, *Whatever you do, do it well*. It cheered me up – its meaning still relevant.

Before falling asleep, I kept repeating Eman's advice for the morning flight: 'Keep calm ... don't push her too hard on take-off ... keep her low.'

I woke up well before five and was glad of the quiet house as I didn't want to see anyone before leaving. I quickly ate a cold breakfast, quietly left the house and set off along my normal route to the airfield. When I was sure I was not being followed, I turned back and headed towards Napajedla.

A few yards after the last house I jumped into the ditch on the right and continued to the back of the factory where I was shielded by tall poplar trees. Everywhere was quiet. A beautiful late summer morning, a skylark already high above. How I envied him!

So far, so good, perhaps too good ... I kept an eye on the time from my hiding place and waited impatiently for the hangar door to open. As the time went by, my tension grew and I kept checking my watch.

0530 hrs.

It was high time to act – fifteen minutes later the first workers started arriving for the morning shift, which also meant two German guards at the gate and German supervision inside the factory. What was going on? We had not allowed for such a delay. What now? I froze with sudden fear, real fear I had never experienced before. So much was at stake! It was quarter to six and the hangar remained firmly shut. Retreat was the name of the game now. My immediate problem was how to get back onto the road, which was already fairly busy. I ran to make up for the lost time as I had to get to the gate in time for the morning shift. I ran past my flat. The idea of hiding the pistol there was not a good one and I just slipped it into my trouser pocket. I reached the gate a few minutes past six.

'Hands up!'

I only escaped trouble from the German guards thanks to the local porter who literally pushed me inside the gate with the words 'Don't hold him back, he's late already.'

19

Only that evening, when I returned the pistol back to Eman, did I learn that our contact had been arrested.

The Germans forgot about our Z-XIII probably due to the start of production of the training planes Klemm 34 and Bucker 181 Bestman. As rumours started circulating that some of us would be sent to Germany for special training, my fear that I was being watched became my constant companion.

A few months later Eman approached me once more. 'You have to leave. They're after you!'

It was the morning shift. To stay until the end and go home was too risky now. I had to act fast. In order to get out of the factory, I claimed a sudden bout of sickness. It worked. The surgery was opposite the railway station, so I sent my three-day sick note back to the factory and left a message for my landlady that I had been sent to Germany to work. An hour later, accompanied by my good friend Alois Baca, we boarded the train heading south to the town of Hodonin close to the Slovak border.

Although we arrived at the town without a hitch, it was not so easy to pick up the promised permits to cross the border into the Slovak State. There were none waiting for us at the address we had been given, but we could not turn back now.

PART TWO

Chapter 2

Direction South

We were lucky. The River Morava which marked the border with Slovakia was frozen solid and we crawled across it quite easily. The only worry was the crunching noise of the snow and the dark silhouettes of the trees.

Suddenly we heard voices – we needed cover and fast! A low wall and a roof of some building behind it appeared out of the fog. We jumped over and found ourselves surrounded by graves. The building was a mortuary. We squatted behind a grave and waited for the sound of the footsteps to die down, then we headed in the opposite direction towards the first Slovak village and walked into the pub. We knew our password: 'Two double slivovice'

The landlord looked up. 'Don't talk, local bobbies are patrolling nearby.'

As soon as he finished, his wife ran into the bar, whispered to him and promptly took us both into the kitchen.

'They are coming ... quick!'

She led us through the back yard and garden, and bid us farewell. 'God be with you.'

We found ourselves on the road to the local railway station.

The train was full of workers, badly lit and smoky. Lojza Baca and I sat apart and reached the city of Bratislava without any further problems. According to our instructions we had to change money at ticket office number five, but it was closed. A few taxi drivers hovered around talking in German. We had to get out of here quickly – I handed my papers to Baca.

'Let's meet back here at twelve noon. If I'm not back, you must try and make it on your own.'

When the next train arrived the platforms and waiting room filled with passengers. The taxi drivers left and I knocked on the shutter. It opened, I uttered the password, but instead of money a voice said, 'Round the corner, ticket office number two, grey haired gentleman.'

I knocked at number two. The shutter opened and a young ginger-haired man who spoke German appeared. What now? I spotted my target inside.

'Excuse me, I'd like to speak to the gentleman behind you,' I said in Czech, pointing at the grey-haired man. He came over and in reply to my password whispered, 'I can't help you now. Wait until twelve.'

It was almost noon. Lojza Baca was waiting too. I had to risk it, so I waited as well. At five minutes past twelve the ginger-haired man reappeared. What did he want?

'Come with me,' he said quietly. 'When I push you, please don't resist.'

He took me over to the ticket offices and out of the blue pushed me through one of the doors, behind which stood the grey-haired man. He quickly exchanged my old money for Slovak crowns and Hungarian pengo and issued appropriate instructions.

Baca was still waiting but we did not board our train until dark, our direction the Hungarian border. We got off at Petrzalka and found our safe house, with another fourteen escapees inside.

We did not stay long, moving on after midnight, snowdrifts and frozen streams everywhere. We staggered along, an icy wind blasting our faces. As we approached a Hungarian village, the howl of dogs grew louder. At one particular house they woke up our next guide, who was expecting only a third of us, so demanded an extra pengo from everybody. He got what he asked for and we set off again. When we reached the railway station we hid behind a stack of straw bales, gave our Hungarian guide the money for the tickets and waited. It did not take him long before he was back – with four policemen, who marched us into the railway station building where we joined another six. They searched us, took our penknives and firearms, and escorted us to the police station where there was another search, followed by interrogation. After two hours they took us back to the border.

The old Slovak guard on duty refused to take us back as, according to some strange rule, there were too many of us. The Hungarian policemen marched us out of sight of the border sentry box, pointed their guns at us and herded us into the nearest wood, still in Slovak territory.

The other escapees disappeared into the darkness leaving Baca and I alone ... no, not quite. Behind us an old man struggled with a huge suitcase so we helped him – after all, we did not know where to turn next and we did not want to leave the cover before dark. We hid behind another stack of bales until the evening. Our newly acquired friend invited us in return to the parish of Pusta Fedymosz just inside Hungary where he knew an evangelical priest who would definitely help us, he claimed.

Under cover of darkness we headed towards the parish. The old man went ahead, pointed out the direction to the parsonage and promised to wait for us there. We took it in turns to carry his heavy suitcase and tried not to lose sight of him. There were a lot of people about as it was Twelfth Night.

He suddenly turned into a narrow side lane and disappeared. We speeded up, turned the corner ... the lane led into the fields ... sounds of steps behind. Where to now? And what about that suitcase?

I spotted a small gate in the wall and pulled Baca and the suitcase in. We found ourselves in a tiny courtyard. The footsteps on the other side of the wall grew louder on the frozen ground. Somebody stopped just outside our gate, it opened and the man stepped in and introduced himself. He was none other than our priest. What a relief! Inside we found the owner of the suitcase and a few others.

At four in the morning we crossed the border again, headed for the local railway station and stopped some distance away from it. The priest went to get the tickets but came back empty-handed. The station was apparently full of police so Baca and I decided to do it our own way. For an hour we crawled in the snow towards the rails and for another hour waited for the train to arrive. When it did we boarded the train from our hideout and persuaded the conductor to sell us the tickets for a little extra. We were on our way to Budapest. The few Hungarian words we had learned from the friendly priest served us well.

We eventually reached the French Consulate without any further mishaps. It was crowded with escapees, but at last my turn came. I was given an address to stay at and was promised that as a pilot I would soon be sent to France. Four days later a messenger from the Consulate came to see me and I signed a receipt for 200 pengo, which I never saw. But I was given a ticket from Budapest to Szeged, where a guide, who would take a group of us – a major, a pilot Svarc, Baca and myself – to Yugoslavia, would meet us.

When we arrived in Szeged our guide wasn't there, but we knew that he had arranged for a taxi driver who would be carrying a green overprinted newspaper as identification. Having decided to find him ourselves, the taxi driver soon arrived and, as both his and our instructions tallied, we got in the car.

We arrived that evening at a solitary farm, only to find that the farmer was suspicious, although he eventually let us in after some haggling and double pay – no wonder, for only a few days earlier the police had caught him sheltering some other hopefuls and he was worried.

We slept on straw on the floor while he took up his position near the range and his wife and child in the opposite corner.

At dawn we headed south on sledges, stopping after about two hours near a village which we were supposed to avoid. The Yugoslav border was on the other side. All we had to do was go through a small wood but when we stepped out of it, we were surrounded by Hungarian border guards and a number of civilians who took us at gunpoint to the guardroom. Meanwhile the Yugoslav border guards stood a few yards away, unable to help.

Chapter 3

Escape from the Citadel

During that first half of January the temperature often dropped to 30° centigrade below zero. There were no windows in the cell of the Szeged prison and only a tiny opening in the door let in a glimpse of light. From next door we heard the screams of some gypsy women. In the corner was the inevitable bucket and there was one bare wooden bed, much too small for four men – my first prison bed. When any of us needed to turn over during the night, the rest had to follow suit.

Each morning started with interrogation. After eleven days on bread and water they returned most of our things and ordered us to stand in the corridor. Much to our surprise, there were thirty-seven altogether, all looking as dishevelled as us. They took us to the nearest barracks and locked us up in the cellar. A tiny window high up let in cold air and some light, while the concrete floor was covered with old straw from military palliasses. At first we were reluctant to lie down on it and agreed to spend the night hanging on to each other, but the cold and fatigue got the better of us.

Next morning a small bowl of some warm liquid and two pieces of bread marginally restored our hopes. By the time they escorted us to the railway station the next day, we were all infested with lice and a number of us had inflamed eyes.

Our next stop was the town of Hodmezovasarhely. Armed guards took us into a low building nearby where we had to hand over all our possessions temporarily. The ground floor was taken up by the guards, with we prisoners on the first floor, where we met another twenty Czechs, amongst them a woman. All windows had had the handles removed and were boarded up, but compared to our previous lodgings we felt much better. We could even have a wash every day and shave once a week, and we took it in turns to cut each other's hair, but despite all that relative luxury, the first signs of scabies appeared and spread fast.

Our despair was growing. It was almost the end of February and we were still stuck in Hodmezovasarhely, so we started planning our escape. We could not get out onto the street, which was guarded, but we had an idea.

In one of the rooms we occupied was a door that lead into the Commandant's office. Every weekend he used to come back from a night out on the town fairly inebriated, which played right into our hands.

I found an old rusty key and altered it using my nail file so that we could open his room. One barred window led into the inner yard – that was the way out! With a filed hook acting as a screwdriver, Baca and a few willing pairs of hands made ropes out of the sheets. We spent the whole week in feverish preparations and although not everyone agreed to the escape, the majority were in favour.

That fateful March Sunday evening, the Commandant took much longer to leave, boring us rigid with his stories about how he got his medals during the First World War. At last he left. Once the guards had checked us over and locked the door, we got ready. At ten o'clock I unlocked the door to the Commandant's office and un-screwed the bars from the window. All went well as first five men and then the woman got out. The next in line, a young medical student, dropped a piece of saved-up bread which hit the metal roof below. Dogs started barking and the guards sounded the alarm. Our hope of escape was gone.

The student returned three weeks later, bruised all over. Our captors were convinced that we had had inside help and it seemed certain we would be moved again.

On Good Friday they took us under escort us to Budapest. It was getting light and when we stopped high on a hill, in front of a huge fortress – the Citadel – the view of the city and the River Danube was beautiful. A trickle of filthy water trailed from underneath the massive gates.

The guard rang the bell, the gates opened and thick fog greeted us. From the first courtyard they let us in one by one across the drawbridge. I was second to go in and was surprised that the guards were not interested in our possessions or money. In the darkened corridor I was met by a roar and several bearded individuals hugged me. I could barely recognize my old friends.

There were about 120 Czechs imprisoned there, with a similar number of Poles housed next door. They were better off as they were allowed parcels from the locals, but despite the strict regulations, they shared everything with us.

We slept on a stone floor, on one huge straw mattress. Inside the building was a big wrought-iron structure, known as the roulette. Several horror tales were told ... it lead into some underground channel from which the noise of running water and scores of rats could be heard. Nobody enjoyed going past it on their way to the toilet block during the night.

On Easter Sunday the Czechs and Poles organized a show. Our old spirit of Sokol could not be suppressed. The Hungarian Commandant liked our performance of physical exercises, as a reward for which we were allowed to take a group photograph and prolonged our stay in the main courtyard. Some took advantage of this by hiding in the ramparts and escaping during the night. The missing Czechs were replaced at roll call by willing Poles as the guards never counted their numbers.

Lice followed the scabies we brought in with us. I suffered especially badly and eventually, after the intervention of an interned Polish doctor, I was allowed treatment outside the gates, in a military hospital, always escorted by two guards. I had to go there three times for treatment with a sulphur solution. My last visit to the hospital was scheduled for Saturday, 30 March, the same day as a planned mass escape from the Citadel.

For us Czechs, the longer we stayed, the more dangerous it became as we had found out that the plan was to hand us over to the Gestapo. This is what actually happened, the planned escape did not take place and anybody who did not get away while at the border ended up in a concentration camp.

I made my mind up to try and escape during my last trip to the hospital. In order not to jeopardize the mass escape plans, I asked the escape committee for permission to do so, and they duly gave it to me, together with a list of various tasks I could do for them once I was out.

It was lovely spring morning when my two guards and I made our way down the hill, my pyjamas stuck to my sulphur-covered body. I wore a suit over those, an overcoat on top of that and my neck scarf – my talisman. It would surely bring me luck today.

As we walked I went over each part of my plan, wondering at which point it would be best to make my escape. One thing puzzled me: today's trip was not taking as long as it usually did.

As we waited in the hospital the guards dozed off. Slowly, step by step, I started walking away from them, pretending to take an interest in the pictures on the wall. I reached the opposite end of our corridor and did not know what to do next as there wasn't another picture round the corner! One more step would get me into the main hospital corridor, but at that moment my name was called and I had to go back.

Well, I would have to try on the way back.

I was determined to grab any chance coming my way, but none did. My head was spinning. As we went past the local chemist I decided to buy some painkillers. Pointing to my head I entered the shop. My attempt to mix with other people did not work as the guards were watching and soon pointed me in the right direction.

It was almost noon, the sun was getting warm, the guards were sweating with the heat and I with agitation. We reached a small square with a wine bar. It took some doing to persuade the guards to go in but there was a shapely barmaid, and one glass of wine was soon followed by second – they were only human after all.

The main gateway led into the back yard and to the toilets at the far end. The first time one of the guards went with me. I ordered brandy and gave them ten pengo, suggesting they should settle the bill while I nip to the toilet once more before we go.

By the time they had decided who would do what, I was out in the square and jumping into the first taxi.

'*Bitte ... schnell.*'

The taxi driver fortunately understood my pigeon German but had to use the starting handle. The guards appeared at the door and headed straight for my taxi. I kept urging '*Schnell... schnell!*' so he could not hear them and we got away.

I gave the driver the address of the flat where I had stayed before; it was in a narrow street behind the French Consulate. I only had five pengo in my pocket and the meter read more. The driver stopped at the corner and as he got out to check the address I put my last money on the seat and disappeared in the crowd. A few minutes later I managed to get past the patrolling policeman inside the French Consulate and breathed a sigh of relief.

I was safe now.

But my joy did not last long – the Consulate clerk refused to help.

'We cannot do anything for you now. Come back another time.'

'Should I return to the Citadel then?'

He changed his tune. The only place he could offer was a dark corner behind the lift. By that evening there were six of us, two women and four men. Somebody came in saying there were two Hungarian guards and a taxi driver outside the door, the driver demanding the rest of the money. The clerk paid the driver … the guards were in for a long wait.

About nine that evening we left the building through the back door. A car was waiting with two people already in it – the driver and the guide. After my previous experience I was suspicious and asked for details of the planned border crossing. It paid off as he disappeared at the next petrol station.

The car drove us across the Hungarian plain which was flooded from the melting snow. It was after two in the morning before we reached our destination, whereupon the driver turned the car round and left. We were on our own. I split the group into pairs and made off first with one of the women, the silence broken only by the sound of our splashing feet. We were in mud up to our ankles.

According to what we'd been told we should avoid the village and go as far as the stream – difficult to find in all that water. Fortunately I made out some willows and the faint silhouette of a small bridge, the far end of which was our target – Yugoslavia, where I had wanted to be three months before.

I walked faster still. The mud was no better on the other side of the bridge, but we did not mind anymore – we were on friendly soil.

Something moved. I froze and so did the others. Nothing, so we carried on.

'*Stoj!*' (Halt!)

31

The voice broke the silence, but the scream of my lady companion was even louder. She freaked out.

'*Kto tamo?*' (Who goes there?)

Now we knew. This was Yugoslavia. At long last ...

'Czechoslovaks,' I shouted happily.

We were made very welcome in their guardroom and treated as friends should be – with hot milk and bread.

Chapter 4

Next Stop France

Even though I was still a long way away from France, my situation was very different and I felt like a tramp who had returned home after a long journey.

In the town of Subotica, where we were taken by a horse-drawn carriage, the local commander tried to persuade me to join the Yugoslav Air Force. But my mind was made up: I wanted to join our resistance and at that time it only existed in France. Two days later we reached the town of Osijek with its large Czechoslovak minority. We were free ...

I carried on to Belgrade by train the next morning, substantially refreshed, and walked from the station to my final destination – Czechoslovak House. More interrogations and tests, then to the doctor to rid me of the lice and scabies. After a few days I felt like a human being again.

We swore our allegiance and joined the Czechoslovak armed forces abroad. On the 6 April 1940 a large group of volunteers left Belgrade by train, our journey taking us via Skopje, along the River Vardar and towards the border with Greece. Salonika – from where the two prophets Cyril and Method had come to my native Moravia in the Middle Ages – was a sharp reminder of my home. View followed view and soon home was but a distant memory. The route took us along the coast of the Aegean Sea, through narrow valleys, steep slopes and endless tunnels, the dark waters of the sea on our left. We went past Alexandropolis, Edirne and the train still carried on ... so much to take in for somebody who had never been abroad before ...

Eventually we reached Istanbul. We looked in amazement from our hotel windows at the sleek minarets and watched the busy life below. We were not allowed out as we were travelling on a special mass pass, so had no documents of our own. But the desire to see the place was strong. We got out through the downstairs window and our willing waiter became our guide – this time a reliable one. He took us along the narrow streets of the poorest part of the town, the only lights coming out of the cheap brothels. We visited some bars and nightclubs in the more affluent part of town and on the way back walked onto the bridge which joins Europe and Asia, but the guard in the middle prevented us from stepping onto the soil of the biggest continent.

Early next morning a small steamer took us across the Bosporus. The view of Istanbul from the deck was breathtaking – the minaret spires pierced the blue sky; the huge white walls of the palaces and their golden domes glittered in the morning sun ... Goodbye Europe ...

We continued our journey on Asian soil. The train sped through a poor hilly area to Ankara, across the Taurus mountain range, and carried on over the wide plains near Adana. French guards took care of us at the Syrian border. After a brief stop in Halab we progressed through a vast emptiness, broken only by an occasional caravan of camels and mules. At Rayak we had to get off the train and boarded a funicular railway. The engine laboured upwards into the hills of Lebanon.

We saw the kind of contrasts one can only find in the Orient as the train went through villages with hoards of children begging. Skinny women with babies in their arms stood silently watching, poverty everywhere.

Suddenly we caught our first glimpse of Beirut, one of the biggest ports of the Mediterranean, and held our breath. On one side of the railway were opulent white villas amongst rows and rows of orange and lemon trees, and on the other side steep slopes of the mountains, their tops covered in snow. At our feet was the capital of Lebanon.

We were put up in the Foreign Legion barracks on the outskirts of the town. The officers were in a hotel with a view of the sea. We had to be back at nine, the same as back home. Three of us got our heads and money together, bribed the commander of our barracks, a German legionnaire, and set off to explore the city. We saw dingy smoking rooms full of hairy locals squatting beside their hookahs, their spitting the only sound; we saw belly dancers in the night-clubs, swaying to the rhythm of oriental music.

34

The next day we enjoyed a good swim in the sea before heading off into the nearby hills. The soil was very rocky and, apart from the occasional tree, only cacti and snakes flourished. We met locals wearing just a strip of loincloth. All this was so new to us – even the sunset was different from at home. As soon as the sun went down, it was pitch dark and we could hardly find the way back. We spotted a bright light ahead of us which turned out to be a local bar full of drunken Senegalese in uniform. They surrounded us and before we realized their intentions, they split us up. It felt like being caught by a giant octopus. They were homosexual as many of the Foreign Legion members were, but we got away – being sober was our biggest advantage. Only when we returned to the barracks did we realize how lucky we were that night.

17 April 1940. In the harbour, cranes had almost completed loading the ocean-going liner *Patria*. Heavy black smoke poured out of her three chimneys. Eventually the passengers, mainly French colonial soldiers of various skin colours, but including 160 Czechoslovaks, stopped milling about. We were ready to sail.

The ship silently slipped her anchor, her big stern breaking the waves and a trail of white foam in her wake. We lost sight of Beirut but stayed on deck well into the night, so fascinating for us was the sea. Only the increasing cold forced us to our accommodation quarters – on the fourth deck below. That put a stop to our dreams from above – long rows of double bunks, poor-quality mattresses and no sheets in sight. With the lights on all night and the increasing cold, there was little chance of any sleep.

Our officers were accommodated on the first deck. The food was quite good but as we were not given any money we couldn't even buy ourselves a cup of tea costing four francs. I came up with the idea to ask our officers for the pay which we had signed for back in Belgrade. According to them we would not receive it until we reached French soil. 'But aboard the liner we are already on French soil,' was my argument.

Why didn't I keep my mouth shut? As the originator of this idea, the men elected me as one of the two spokesmen. Admittedly I was still wearing a reasonably good-looking suit, albeit adorned by a pair of old and suspect-looking grey plimsolls.

We climbed up to the first deck. The foyer of the dining room was so posh that I felt out of place. Through the glass doors we saw our officers lounging in comfortable armchairs, ice buckets with bottles of champagne at hand. That boosted my courage. I stopped the first waiter and with my broken French asked to speak with the gentlemen inside.

It took a while before two of them even got up. As they went past us, I stood to attention and acknowledged them, but they took no notice and headed for the toilets. That was a bit much!

On their way back I intercepted them and without further ado presented our case. One of them, a major, started yelling at me that I had no right to be on the first deck. The other one, the officer in charge, promised to send his subordinates to talk to us. We reported back to our friends.

Later, two junior officers turned up and informed us that our commanders had decided to pay us four francs a day so that we would have enough money left to buy our kit in France. My adrenalin must have still been high as I replied, 'We're not mercenaries and don't have to buy our own kit!'

I followed this up by suggesting that we should demand the full pay due to us, everybody agreed and the two officers left.

Nothing happened. My next move was to present our case to the ship's captain, who was French. I needed an interpreter for that and found a willing volunteer in a Mr Hora.

We were met on the bridge by the captain's second in command wanting to know the purpose of our visit. When he took us in, I was quite taken back by the towering presence of the bearded French captain. He listened carefully to our plea and suggested that those who were feeling fine should lend their blankets to those worse off. I pointed out that we had no blankets at all, at which point he lost his patience and shouted, 'Who is your commanding officer? I want him here! Now!'

A few minutes later the captain's second in command brought our senior officers in.

'You call yourselves officers and you are not capable of looking after a hundred of your own men? There are thousands of other soldiers aboard my ship and they all are looked after well!'

Our officers left with their tails between their legs. I almost pitied them. We got the blankets shortly after that, but it was quite obvious that this would not be forgotten.

Shortly afterwards we were ordered onto the first deck. We stood three men deep, our officers in the far corner. Their spokesman, a major, repeated the offer of four francs a day and asked for a show of hands. None went up. He continued, 'Very well then. You will get all your money. But we consider Siska's actions a mutiny and he will be arrested and imprisoned as soon as we reach France.'

I put up my hand and said, 'Mutiny means that officers are thrown overboard. So far, you all are still here ...'

The men found it amusing; the officers did not.

A lot of men monopolized the ship's canteen for some time afterwards.

The ship stopped in Alexandria for a few hours and the captain agreed for selected soldiers to be allowed ashore. I joined the queue with my mind made up not to return to the ship. My logic was that France was at war and badly needed pilots. I had with me my operational pilot's licence and, more importantly, a certified copy of it in French as well.

But it did not matter. The two officers issuing the permits refused to let me go. My mind was made up and I found a solution – after dark I simply climbed down onto the quay along the anchor chain.

It all went smoothly – too smoothly, in fact. I paused on the quay to get my bearings and that cost me dearly. The guards approached me and promptly escorted me back to the ship.

The two officers were still on duty and the looks on their faces when they saw me coming back was worth the effort ...

After putting in to Alexandria and Algeria we sailed past Sardinia and the Balearics where we were hit by a severe storm. It was dark and the sea heaved and heaved. The *Patria* became a toy at its mercy as huge waves engulfed the deck. We could barely stay in our beds and that night's dinner was left largely uneaten.

On the eighth day, 25 April, under a cloudless sky, we reached Marseille where trucks took us to the barracks of the Foreign Legion at the Fortress Saint Jean. Those who could read French spotted the sign above the gate: 'You legionnaires are soldiers destined to die and I am sending you to the place of dying.' Those, to whom this was addressed, stood impassively around.

After the usual roll call we still had time to have a quick look around the harbour and the town, and consume several glasses of red wine. We had to spend the night in the barracks and had only just switched the lights off when the swatting noises started and somebody shouted, 'Switch that light on!' Never in my life had I seen so many cockroaches. The ceiling was completely covered with them and they showered down on us. As we ran out in a blind panic, the seasoned legionnaires laughed their heads off. We would get used to it, they said. We spent the rest of the night on our blankets – outside in the courtyard.

We were relieved to leave the next day by train to Names, and the same afternoon via Montpellier to the small seaside town of Agde, our next port of call. A Czech brass band greeted our arrival. We were billeted under canvas near the Canal du Midi, in a camp previously inhabited by members of the Spanish international brigades.

At roll call we were separated according to our qualifications. I ended up with the air force group where I met six members of my old 8 Squadron, including my commanding officer. While we were waiting to join the French forces, we spent our time rehearsing military drill, long marches and guard duties. My kit consisted of a pair of overalls and no boots. For sentry duty we borrowed the discarded kit of Alpine troops. Our firearms were old First World War muskets with a long barrel and one bullet. Daily pay was fifty centimes and a glass of beer cost three times as much. I should add at this point that the stupid affair on the *Patria* had been forgotten.

On the day we arrived at Agde, the German Army reached Oslo.

The fighting went on in northern Norway and rumours circulated about our possible deployment above the Arctic Circle. Before this could happen, however, we received the next bit of news. On 10 May the Nazis invaded Belgium and Holland.

I reported for front-line duty, but I was still stuck in Agde and my miserable mood was not even elevated by my promotion to the rank of Sergeant, and the repeated reporting for duty. The only comfort was the reports brought in by the occasional visitors – Czechoslovak fighter pilots who were successfully engaged in fighting, but also at the cost of our first heavy losses.

Our air force group was posted to the Merignac airfield near Bordeaux at the beginning of June. At last we were in the proper place. We wanted to join in the fighting as soon as possible, but our hopes were dashed by the worrying news from the front.

The Germans had stormed into northern France and after successfully breaching the line at Sedan, reached the Channel on 20 May. They progressed fast. The south of the country was in turmoil, with roads and harbours crammed with fleeing civilians and soldiers alike. It was anybody's guess how far the Germans would get.

One afternoon, out of the clear sky, came two flights of German bombers. The first bombs hit the hangars and other buildings, and we had our first casualties. I escaped with only a broken arm and was taken to hospital. On my return I was sent to our embassy in Bordeaux, together with two other pilots, Messrs Bauman and Pospichal. The embassy had already moved there from Paris, as had other foreign legations. We were given the task of hiding several people in Bata's French factories.

Travelling was difficult, despite our diplomatic number plates and we often had to force our way through the fleeing crowds. By the time we returned to the embassy, the majority of the employees had already fled so we turned round and went back to our airfield, only to find it smashed up and deserted.

We had no choice but to return to the embassy, fighting our way through the crowded streets once more. With the clerks gone, we issued each other with new passports, signing for the ambassador in his absence, and took it in turns in the queue for Spanish visas. They closed the door for good that afternoon. Panic was fast setting in.

On 17 June we listened to the voice of Marshal Petain: 'I regret to inform you all that we now have to lay down our arms ...'

People despaired, panic stricken. When we returned to our own legation we found the cleaner inspecting boxes full of table silver.

'You can take what you want, lady, in exchange for some food.'

Sweet, sweet France ...

We drove to the harbour and pushed the car off the cliff ... we were not alone.

In the late afternoon of 21 June 1940, we managed to force our way aboard a Danish trawler bound for England.

Chapter 5

311 Squadron

We arrived at Falmouth on Monday, 24 June 1940. All the pressure of three days spent squashed, hungry and thirsty below deck, expecting the next torpedo to be aimed at us, disappeared. We were in the land of the living once again. All around us it was calm and clean, a bit like Sunday back home.

We met the famous English calmness at every step. Without delay they took us to the railway station with no pompous speeches, no shouting, no excessive running around or waving hands full of some pointless paperwork.

Women of the British Red Cross and YMCA offered us cigarettes, cakes, lemonade and tea – with a smile. But they wanted something in return – they were asking for a souvenir, the only word we could understand. Those who were not wearing French uniform and could not give a button or a buckle, had to sign a piece of paper at least.

The train was waiting but we were not particularly rushing aboard. On each carriage was a sign, either 'SMOKING' or 'NON SMOKING', but we were not wearing a 'smoking', which in Czech means a dinner jacket. Only after they explained to us that the 'SMOKING' sign was for smokers, we happily boarded the clean and comfortable carriages.

We headed north across fairly plain countryside with neatly cut lawns and hedges. There were not many fields, mainly pastures full of pretty looking cows. All stations' names were painted over, the only reminder of the war.

What do they fight with? we wondered.

We were still asking the same question at our next destination, an airfield in Warrington. Nothing would excite or upset the English unduly, not even the arrival of soldiers from defeated France or the return of their own from Dunkirk. Extensive alterations to the airfield suggested more preparations of 'just in case'... rather than a country fully engaged in war. That's the English for you. The usual response to our agitated requests for a faster pace was 'Take it easy, we'll win the war anyway.'

Where was this belief in their own victory coming from? Did they simply believe in centuries of tradition? According to the old saying they would lose battles but win wars. I did not know, but their composure was a bit unnerving.

We were looked after well in our wooden lodgings. There were a cinema, swimming pool, clubroom and good food, though different from that at home or in France. Milk in the tea took us a long time to get used to, but it was so good I have never stopped drinking it since.

Our next stop on the journey to war was the airfield at Cosford where we arrived two weeks later. There were about a thousand of us – officers and other ranks mixed together. After we had sworn allegiance to the King, we were given our new ranks. Commissioned officers became Pilot Officers, non-commissioned officers became Sergeants and ground crews Aircraftmen 2nd Class. Everybody was issued with two air force blue uniforms, two pairs of boots, two shirts, cleaning kit and, most importantly, new papers, which meant we could go outside the barracks after we had finished our duties. Walking out started at 1830 hrs and finished one minute before midnight – and applied to everyone without exception.

On Saturday afternoons and Sundays we were invited by local families to partake in their weekend activities. We enjoyed these outings very much, though we had to overcome two obstacles: lack of English and beer without a head. We used our hands a lot as we tried hard to compensate for our English inadequacies with a sort of sign language.

Our impatience and concern about our first deployment soon came to an end. On 12 July 1940, the first Czechoslovak squadron was formed, 310 Fighter Squadron, was first deployed in the Battle of Britain on 18 August and passed with flying colours. 312 and 313 Fighter Squadrons soon followed and a Czechoslovak flight was formed within 68 Night Fighter Squadron as well. Many of our pilots flew with English, and some even with Polish, units. Our administration remained in Cosford, though part of it later transferred to Wilmslow.

On 2 August, 311 Czechoslovak Night Bomber Squadron was formed at RAF Honington in East Anglia – our squadron.

The necessary conversion to Wellingtons did not take us long. A few practise take-offs and landings with dual controls on a twin-engine Anson and we were ready. Some of us did not even finish the required number of hours on training flights before joining operational crews. They were told that they would finish the compulsory training later ... a somewhat unorthodox approach but the situation demanded it.

The Battle of Britain was raging.

On Tuesday, 10 September our operational crews took off for their first raid. The target was the railway station in Brussels where the enemy had gathered supplies for the planned invasion of Britain. This day was an historic date as Czechoslovak airman took their fight to enemy territory, amongst the first to fly night operations over Germany.

But who could give us any practical advice in terms of correct height to fly or the avoidance of enemy anti-aircraft fire? Who knew at that time how to drop our bombs correctly, how to spot and avoid German fighters in the dark?

The papers reported this raid as follows:

A recent bombing raid on the railway depot in Brussels was performed with utmost accuracy. The planes flew low through heavy anti-aircraft fire and circled the target as many as four times to aim well. This squadron had a very good reason to fulfil its task as well as possible because it was the Czechoslovak squadron within the RAF, which had its first opportunity to attack Germany. After a mere twenty-four days of training the Czechoslovak airmen wanted to make most of their first operational raid. They succeeded.

We had to – after all we chose as our squadron emblem the Hussite weapons and under the arms of God's soldiers the first three words of the Hussite hymn as our motto: 'Na Množstvi Nehledte!' (Do Not Fear The Numbers!).

King George VI approved this motto in October 1941. Never before had the monarch approved a motto in the Czech language. The emblems for the three fighter squadrons were also approved. 310's emblem was a lion with the motto in English: 'We Fight to Create'. No. 312 chose a stork (modelled on the famous French Squadron known as The Storks, as some of our pilots flew with them), and a Latin motto: *'Non Multa, Sed Multum'*. Finally 313 had a crane and a motto in Czech: *'Jeden jestřáb mnoho vran rozhání'* (One Crane Scares Many Crows).

With intensified operational activity, 311 Squadron suffered its first losses. England's situation at that time was critical. Despite continuous German bombing the country survived and, after the victorious outcome of the Battle of Britain, managed to squash Hitler's planned invasion. It was a significant victory, especially as the enemy was much stronger at that time.

The British Prime Minister Winston Churchill summed up the achievement in his famous speech; 'Never in the field of human conflict was so much owed by so many to so few.'

At the end of 1940 we took delivery of a new mark of Wellington, carried on with our training and welcomed new arrivals. By this time we had relocated to the airfield at East Wretham, a satellite of Honington.

Life during the war became more structured. Apart from the 'special' times when we were on extra duty, we flew on operations (ops), on average, every fourth day. After six operational weeks crews were entitled to ten days' leave, anywhere in Britain.

We often went to London, though the entertainment was sometimes disrupted. The Germans were concentrating their bombing on the city at this time and London found itself in the front line. I was in London with another pilot and friend of mine Ada Musalek during one such raid on 10 May 1941. That evening we had gone into a dance hall near Bloomsbury Square. It was packed, and two bands had their hands full trying to outplay the anti-aircraft fire from the nearby park. As the noise of the approaching German bombers grew louder, so did the intensity of the music.

Anyone who wanted a stiff drink had to cross the street to the bar opposite. Outside it was dark, with the bursts of anti-aircraft shells and German flares creating an eerie atmosphere. This was shattered by a sudden whistling noise followed by a series of explosions in the next street that obliterated everything else. The ground shook and glass starting flying around.

'That was too close. Please go to the nearest shelter,' the night warden kept pleading.

But we preferred the bar which was packed. A few candles provided the only light as the electricity was off. After a while we found empty stools by the bar. Englishmen, patient and weathered by now, only lowered their voices when the bombs were falling.

Could anything at all disrupt their composure?

We did not hear the next bomb, but the explosion was awful. The impact was so great that it blew the candles out and knocked us off our stools.

In the complete darkness a few women screamed but everybody abided by the barman's call: 'Quiet please'. Through the blown-in door we could hear the explosions interspersed by the sound of falling glass and masonry.

We stood there for a while watching this macabre spectacle.

Then we heard another bomber approaching, its engine revs irregular in order to mislead the defence. We watched the sky and wondered where the next load would fall. Out of the darkness came red and white tracer followed by a burst from a fighter's machine gun.

A huge burst of bright light illuminated the sky, followed by another explosion as the bomber took a full hit, burst into flames and quickly disappeared from our vision. What we had seen that night was just a tiny part of the big battle above London.

We returned to the dance hall and carried on.

It was all quiet by the time the dance finished at midnight and we stepped outside. We took the Underground, its vast corridors used not only as shelters, but also as temporary homes for those who had lost their own in the bombing. People slept in the overcrowded corridors and stairs, went to work from there and came back again at night.

Next morning we walked through the neighbourhood. Rescue personnel were digging out the dead and the wounded; fires were still glowing. The newspapers announced the first count: 'One thousand dead! Over two thousand wounded! Thirty-three German bombers destroyed!'

The outcome of one night . . .

Chapter 6

Night Battle

The extent of the destruction we had witnessed on our leave and the news from home filled us with even more determination to get our own back. There wasn't only a handful of us now and more planes were delivered. Hundreds of Allied bombers ventured even deeper into Germany and together repaid Hitler for his dirty deed. The long flights into enemy territory were not easy as the Germans took good care of protecting their own towns and factories.

But we were not alone – the Soviet Union joined in the fight against Germany ...

During the summer of 1941, the main operational activity of No. 3 Group, Bomber Command, of which we were part, focussed on the Ruhr where the enemy concentrated the production of supplies for the Eastern Front.

The nights were moonlit, but the war turned them into hell. We took off as often as every second day to take maximum advantage of the weather. Although we were on our own as a crew, there was some reassurance in seeing so many other planes around us. The Germans began to feel the impact of such intensified bombing.

The concentration of flak and anti-aircraft fire over some targets was so high that not even a stone could get through, we could only see every third of the tracer rounds and the steel cables of barrage balloons threatened to cut off the wings of our planes.

Worst of all were the enemy fighters. After Germany occupied Holland and France, they created a warning system along the coast – all the way from Denmark down to the so-called French State – which was their first line of concentrated anti-aircraft defence.

The second line of defence was the fighter airfields stretching from Denmark and along the German western border. The Germans divided this airspace into small squares. Each airfield had one to look after and a German fighter on standby. As soon as an airfield spotted one of us, the fighter took off in pursuit. It was a well-developed system of land/air co-operation.

The Germans kept altering their tactics to get us to fly through the same airspace within a short time so that, supported by searchlights, the fighters had a good opportunity to attack as many planes as possible.

This was the first part of the German fighter strategy. The second one meant that they waited for us on our return journey and attacked us when we were at our most vulnerable. They correctly assessed our exhaustion and took full advantage of it.

The third line of defence was the searchlights over the Ruhr. As soon as one got hold of us, the fighter took over, fired a red flare and the searchlights went off.

It took a lot of skilful manoeuvring to get away from him once he got us on his radar.

Apart from these active lines of defence, the Germans also devised a few false targets to deviate us from our course. They lit false fires away from our targets, built mock factories and lit up certain open spaces to create the impression of an airfield – all that just to get us to drop the bombs away from the actual targets.

A Wellington crew consisted of six men: the first pilot (the captain of the aircraft), second pilot, navigator, wireless operator and two gunners, front and rear.

My first crew, and the one I later took over, was captained by Ada Musalek, a gentle, rather introverted chap from the northern town of Moravska Ostrava. He was twenty-four at that time and is buried in England. I was the second pilot. The captain usually took off, flew over the target, and if everything went to plan, handed over to the second pilot for the return journey.

Our navigator was Pepa Mohr, a handsome 26-year-old chap from somewhere in the Krkonose Mountains. The wireless operator, Josef Scerba, also from Moravia, was the same age and was noted for his huge blue eyes. Both were officers. Also from Moravia was the front gunner Pavel Svoboda, a law student; he was slim and very thoughtful. The rear gunner was nicknamed Blondy, though his real name was Rudolf Skalicky; he was born in Yugoslavia of Czech parents but he lived with his granny in Prague. He left her at the age of twenty-two to fight the Germans. He was well built, really strong and rather quiet.

Six people, six different characters and backgrounds, who were thrown together by war and their common desire to help defeat Hitler, and to liberate their homeland. We were a good company, always looking out for each other and ready to risk our lives for each other. There wasn't any other way ...

On Tuesday, 12 August 1941 we were on our way back from Hanover, flying KX-M. As we neared the English coastline Blondy's voice came over the intercom: 'Twin-engined plane behind us, same height. Out of range at the moment.'

We acknowledged his message in the cockpit and asked Blondy to keep his eyes focused. We had seen many other planes as the night was clear and we had just completed a big bombing raid over the target. The plane kept its distance behind us so Blondy could not identify it. As we arrived over our own airfield, another plane was just landing below us. The control instructed us: 'M for Marie, one more round. Height 300 feet, second to land.'

'M for Marie, message understood.'

I levelled the plane on the last turn, switched over to the intercom and ordered the gunners to leave their positions – a necessary precaution in case of a crash landing. I switched back to the radio and heard: 'M for Marie, your turn.'

The green light below replaced the red one. All I could see apart from that was a faint line of the landing strip lights.

'Marie,' called the controller, 'switch on your landing lights! Some idiot is behind you and could land on top of you.'

'Understood. What's he playing at? Are we expecting a raid?'

'No, we've already given the all clear.'

I was steering the plane into her last turn when the first white tracers entered the cabin, immediately followed by the sound of the machine gun. Simultaneously somebody shouted, 'He's firing at us!'

A second salvo followed, by which time I was in a sideslip and my hands were full trying to level out just above the ground.

The landing was a bit bumpy and off the strip. We touched down on her belly with no time for undercarriage.

The 'idiot' behind us was a German. He dropped a few bombs for good measure and was off.

Marie was hit forty-seven times. Some bullets passed only a few inches above the gunner's heads in the middle – the Germans knew full well that the gunners had to leave their turrets prior to the landing.

Marie went for repairs and two days later we flew with a new plane, D for Dalibor. After three ops with her we were told on our return from Kiel that there was a German over our airfield.

Having been ordered to leave the plane as soon as we had landed and take cover, we duly landed, the crew got out and I tried to get the plane off the landing strip. I only managed a few yards when several bombs hit the ground behind me, huge explosions that virtually lifted the plane off the ground.

I was taxiing too fast at this point and could not brake sufficiently at the end of the strip so I turned sharply left, towards the trees. One of the wings clipped the bushes and caused some damage, but much more serious damage was discovered next day, all caused by shrapnel.

Two of the crew were hit by flying debris and suffered minor burns, but they rejoined the rest of us almost immediately. Dalibor needed some repairs ...

Continuous bombing caused us a lot of problems, we could not carry on with night training of new arrivals and the airfield needed constant repair. We also spent hours after each raid clearing up spent shrapnel, while civilian employees filled in bomb craters and levelled the ground with steamrollers.

The morning after another raid a Wellington was taking off. Halfway down the take-off strip and to the right was a slowly moving steamroller with a two-man crew. The plane's wheel caught a piece of shrapnel, the tyre burst and the plane swung sharply to the right, hitting the steamroller and causing the fuel tanks to burst on impact ... the stench of burning flesh lingered over the whole airfield for several days.

Chapter 7

The Long Flights

We were given a new plane, F for Felix, and on Sunday, 7 September 1941 we took off to bomb Berlin. Our target was Goering's Ministry of Aviation, allegedly the biggest one in the world. Berlin as a target was not an easy one as most of the flight was over German territory.

It was a beautiful autumn night. The engines revelled in the cold air, although we were slow gaining height due to the heavy bomb load.

In the distance we could see some flashes making it difficult to choose the right spot for crossing the Dutch coast, but we had to make a decision soon as our heavy load would not allow for any sharp manoeuvring later.

The surf below indicated the coastline and although the flashes increased we still felt well out of the reach of any anti-aircraft fire. As we crossed the coastline at 3,000 feet, the tension was palpable.

The first warning came from our front gunner Pavel Svoboda.

'Steer left – balloons!'

The plane shook as the first puffs of smoke appeared on our right – we were right in a network of barrage balloons! Ada Musalek turned towards the puffs and they followed us for some time after that.

'River below,' reported Pavel.

'That must be the Rhine ... those flashes to the left will be Cologne.'

'Ada, course zero five zero, direct to Berlin?' asked the navigator Pepa Mohr.

We were still climbing very slowly.

The flak around Kassel was more concentrated but we managed to steer clear of it. It was much worse at Magdeburg where we had to fly through a band of searchlights, but by now we had used some of our fuel and so could fly higher and manoeuvre more easily.

At 12,000 feet we switched on our oxygen.

No sooner had we got out of reach of the Magdeburg defence than we were welcomed by the defensive ring around Berlin. First the night fighters, followed by searchlights and flak. If only we could have been just spectators ...

We began to sweat despite the temperature reaching almost minus 30° centigrade, and the heating did not work. Scores of searchlight beams criss-crossed ahead of us, followed by a large number of explosions. Those caught in the searchlight beams had no chance of escaping alive. If only this had been just a show ...

Numerous flares marked Berlin by now as bombs exploded and fires raged far below us.

At last we reached our target. Pepa in his role of bomb-aimer requested a slight change of course. Shells were exploding everywhere as yellow and blue searchlight beams searched for their next victim. The intense light blinded us. I tried to shield Ada's eyes so he could see the instruments – we could not afford any mistakes now.

Wireless operator, bomb-aimer and even us pilots all had our hands full, but what about our gunners in their exposed turrets? They saw most of the action but maintained silence. They had no choice – they knew full well that we had to keep to our exact course.

Pepa broke the silence.

'Bombs gone.'

The plane lifted slightly and in the rear turret Blondy started counting: 'One, two, three. All exploded.'

Wireless operator Josef Scerba reported back to England that we had dropped our bombs at 2315 hrs and Pepa Mohr took the obligatory photograph of the target.

'Ada, it's all done. Let's get out of here!'

The engines roared and the plane shook. We tried to prevent the Germans from monitoring our position by desynchronizing the engines.

As we left the target area it became relatively peaceful and I took over the controls for the return journey. The plane was much lighter and was easier now to manoeuvre. I turned to the darkest part of the sky and set the homeward course.

I soon started feeling unusually tired so I checked the oxygen supply, which read zero. I tried the regulator but nothing happened. The rest of the crew were also without oxygen.

'I'll go and have a look,' said Mohr, and shortly reported a damaged pipe next to the cylinders.

The altimeter read 20,000 feet and our sweat-soaked clothing was getting cold. I had a sweet taste in my mouth and all I wanted to do was sleep; my head was spinning and my lungs felt like two lumps of ice.

I set the course of two seven zero and into a gradual descent.

The shells were exploding around us ... my eyes were heavy. I was cold and felt as if I were shrinking ...

'Switching to autopilot ...'

Nobody replied or were my ears blocked?

Ahead of us a shell exploded ... did it hit us?

I could not remember anything else until my head hit the instrument panel and I woke up. With my hands neatly folded in my lap, the joystick was moving on its own.

I grabbed it but it was stiff – only then did I remember that we were flying on autopilot.

'Pepa, where are we?'

No response.

'Hey chaps, what's up with you?'

The clock in front of me read ten past two. We had been asleep for almost three hours.

The crew started coming round. We were at 6,000 feet and the air was well oxygenated. We had no idea where we were.

Scerba requested our position from Hull, who told us that we were over Holland. Just then the anti-aircraft fire started again ...

We eventually landed safely and after two days of coughing blood we took off again. We had no choice, it was a special one ...

10 September 1941. Three experienced crews were chosen to bomb Turin. Wellingtons had not been as far as Italy before as the maximum range on their normal fuel tanks wasn't enough, so special cigar-shaped auxiliary fuel tanks had to be suspended under our aircraft, each holding twenty gallons. After the other crews left the

briefing room, our Squadron Commander, Lieutenant Colonel Josef Ocelka, issued the orders.

'Take off at 1845 hrs on main fuel tanks as usual. At 3,000 feet switch over to the auxiliary tank. After two hours switch back to the main tanks and ditch the empty auxiliary. Don't forget or you won't be able to open the bomb door. Understood? You will fly over both free and occupied France. Now, pay attention. Those of you who have not climbed to 9,000 feet by the time you reach the town of Chambery will turn back – you won't make it over the Alps otherwise. Your secondary target is Le Havre. Understood? Good luck!'

The navigators packed their gadgets and we all went for tea.

That night we took off first. Those with targets nearer home took off several hours later.

The rest of the crews came to see us off, especially the other pilots. They were curious to see how we were going to get off the ground. So were we. But it worked and we crossed the shores of England at dusk. The climb took longer than ever.

I was at the secondary controls and kept my eyes on the fuel supply. We ditched the extra tank after two hours and as we climbed above the clouds we could see the white alpine peaks rising above the cloud level in far distance. The cloud cover got thinner nearer the mountains. Below us was the silver streak of the River Rhone and the long lake near Chambery, which was lit up. We were over the so-called Free French State.

'We are at 7,000 feet and we have got 300 gallons of fuel left. What now?'

Nobody replied but everyone had the same thought: are we turning back? Who would believe that we had not reached the required height? And what was it like on the other side of the Alps? They only chose three crews ...

The first pilot increased the revolutions and suggested, 'We could try ...'

With the Alps getting ever closer, we climbed steeply, making for the nearest visible saddle.

I looked at the engine temperature. The needles were almost touching red. All vents were fully open, but even so the rings around the exhaust pipes were glowing.

The snowy tops were everywhere as we reached the saddle. Sharp alpine peaks sprouted around us menacingly. The plane was held up by her propellers – just one engine blip and that would be the end of us.

At last, as we flew into darkness, the snowy peaks disappeared, and the captain was able to reduce the revs to normal flying speed. We breathed a sigh of relief.

To find Turin was going to be easy as they didn't bother much with blackout. There was plenty of flak but judging by the tracer their aim was not very good.

We fired the flares, dropped the bombs and I took over for the journey back.

High up over the Alps on the Italian side they attempted to fire at us ... one last glance at the snow-covered peaks and we were back over France. The wireless operator switched off the radio to avoid accidentally transmitting – the Germans could always identify us and send up the fighters.

The clouds dispersed and the side wind increased.

'River below and a town as well,' reported the front gunner.

'Navigator, report our position.'

The navigator appeared in the cabin, compared his map with the ground below and said, 'Lyon ... two more hours and we reach the Channel!'

The first pilot took the place of the bomb-aimer. He was not feeling too good.

Pressing the fuel supply button showed 300 gallons. Either it was wrong or we did not have enough fuel to get home. I set the revs on economy. All we could do now was wait. As we disappeared into the clouds again, both engines suddenly cut out and the plane shook.

I told the crew, 'Don't panic ... main tank empty ... we still have sixty gallons in reserve.'

I switched the tanks over and the engines picked up nicely, but we lost several hundred feet of precious height.

Half an hour later we dropped out of the clouds and were able to make out a shoreline below us. Suddenly the sky around us was alive with flash after flash, puffs of black smoke and the inevitable searchlight beams.

We were over Le Havre as strong winds had carried us off course to the south. As soon as we reached the Channel, the engines started misfiring. We went into a glide but that did not help for long, and soon the propellers were turning silently. The altimeter kept dropping and below us was the darkness ...

We were at a mere 900 feet. With my eyes on the front screen I was tumbling into the dark unknown.

'Gunners leave your turrets ... prepare for a landing at sea ... get ready!'

If only I could see that sea.

I was alone in the cabin. The others were waiting inside the fuselage. Suddenly a thin line of foam appeared, growing lighter and lighter.

'Chaps ... England ... the coast!'

I sent out an SOS using the searchlight below the front turret. The beacon light came up and marked our route to an airfield, right on our course.

The first trees appeared in the early morning light. We were getting close. Amongst the trees was a lighter square.

I turned the plane and attempted to line up for a landing. The square grew closer ... it did not look big enough.

I automatically pulled on the undercarriage and the flaps when the plane caught the last tree at the edge of the open ground and was pulled down. Quickly I levelled the plane. There was a succession of loud crashes and I could feel the wings hit something big.

The plane slowed down as the wheels touched the ground. A few more big bumps followed and then we nosedived. At last, all forward movement stopped as the tail hit the ground. Another burst, this time the back wheel. We had landed.

'Everybody out ... we're home!' I shouted. They were all still inside the fuselage trying to balance the weight.

We got out only to discover that our assumed airfield was in fact a meadow covered with huge wooden stakes to prevent the landing of enemy aircraft! Both wings were smashed.

It was barely first light. From the opposite side of the meadow came a few members of the Home Guard and checked our credentials. They were obviously pleased with the outcome of our landing and invited us to the nearby farm for a hearty breakfast.

The commanding officer from the nearest airfield arrived and inspected the plane.

'Who landed this?'

'I did, Sir.'

'Good work, Sergeant. Congratulations.'
'What will happen to the plane, Sir?'
'We'll leave it for now – it's quicker to make a new one.'
After lunch our squadron commander came to take us back.
A few days later I was flying over Hamburg, but in a new aircraft.

Chapter 8

Third Year

Our airfield at East Wretham was in grounds belonging to a Lady Ritchie. The officers stayed in the stately home, while sergeants and other ranks slept at first in the local farm or under canvas, and later in wooden huts. We buried our dead in the local church graveyard. During time off we went swimming in the lake or fishing, and although pheasants and rabbits were off limits ...

We particularly liked cycling, and not just for fitness. As soon as we disappeared into the local woods, all our tensions eased as we cycled along without talking, listening to the silence. We enjoyed the smell of heather, clover and ripening brambles. Sometimes we heard a splash, birdsong and even a grasshopper. Nature had a calming effect. We wanted to live and the war felt far away.

Would it all come to an end one day? When would we have peace again?

The sight of the watchtowers and ominous barrels of the anti-aircraft guns always brought us back to reality ...

I was trying to get some sleep after one raid – something which usually took a while – and had just nodded off when I was woken up.

'Very sorry, Mr Siska, but the cooks refuse to cook today's meat ration. Would you be kind enough to go and have a look, please?'

The English corporal in charge of food deliveries for our mess was standing by my bed. This wasn't the first time and, as the elected president of the Sergeants' Mess, I had to deal with it – not a job to be envied during the war.

In the kitchen, the usual pleasant aroma was overshadowed by the stench of old meat. Mutton again – big ribs of Australian mutton which did not look appetizing.

56

We were growing tired of mutton, it was served too often and there was nowhere we could buy any extras.

I asked for a meeting with the Quartermaster Sergeant and the Wing Commander, both of whom duly arrived and we engaged in a lengthy discussion. The Quartermaster Sergeant argued that the weight of the meat was correct and that even the Prime Minister would not get any more. I readily agreed, but when I pointed out the poor quality of the meat he wavered, so I picked up a rib and shoved it under his nose.

Half an hour later we received a fresh ration and I could go back to bed. Everyone can make mistakes, but the British were swift in putting them right.

The building of our new mess was almost finished; we only had to furnish it and get some cutlery, then we could all eat together.

We wanted to turn the old Mess, a wooden hut, into a clubhouse. The corporal and I drove to Norwich and in the local department store ordered all the things we needed at a cost of several hundred pounds. We had no money with us and nobody knew us, but my Czech signature on the receipt was enough. Trust is a wonderful thing ...

Sunday, 20 September. We were due over Italy again, this time Genoa, as part of a multi-target raid.

It had to be said that ops over Italy weren't particularly 'profitable' due to the distance. However, it was important that Mussolini was given to understand that he was vulnerable even on the other side of the Alps, and that it did not pay to send his bombers over somebody else's country.

We took off first, at twilight, the engines of our new Wimpy, B for Bozena, purring happily. On her side were painted new letters: KX-B. We flew into a storm before we left the English coast which caused the intercom to crackle so badly that we could hardly understand each other. Electrical sparks from the propellers created a continuous ring, several feet wide. Anything metallic was discharging.

Scerba had to switch the radio off as he could not make out what was being said by our controller.

'Pavel, why are you firing?'

'I'm not ... they're sparks in between the barrels.'

'Same here,' reported Blondy.

'What a mess,' the captain mused.

We hoped the Bosch would leave us alone so that we could carry on observing the unusual phenomenon. We ditched the empty auxiliary tank and started climbing faster.

The weathermen had got it wrong this time – we had no idea where we were and we'd been flying for hours.

As the first stars appeared, snow-covered Alpine peaks were projected against the ink-coloured sky. We flew through a saddle, majestic glaciers on either side, then a while later, Turin. There seemed to be no activity anywhere. How come they were not firing at us?

Eventually they did fire and with some effort, but we dropped our bombs and set course for home. The storm over France had abated, the transmission improved and Scerba could make radio contact. It took him a while to come off the air, but he told us, 'They're asking where we were. They thought we were shot down.'

It appeared that all RAF operations had been cancelled due to bad weather. As we had had to switch our radio off so soon after take-off, we did not get the recall and so we were the only RAF crew which completed the task.

'They want us to land at Manston as our airfield is fog bound,' Scerba reported.

With the cloud base at 300 feet, we dropped below the clouds over the Channel. We were in a pea souper.

'Manston can't take us either,' came the next bit of news. 'Abington is our next stop. Course Two Two Zero.'

Minutes felt like eternity.

At last we were over the airfield and got permission to land. It was dark below but we were out of the fog.

'Lights below on the left,' came from the front gunner.

'I can see them, but the landing strip is so short . . .'

I was approaching the lights and dropped down. The row of lights suddenly swerved and we spotted a convoy of lorries and trees. Yes, a convoy of lorries. Full throttle and quickly up again.

I switched over to the radio, asked the controller for permission to land and the flarepath to be switched on.

The controller replied, 'Permission to land. Direction Two Nine Zero.'

We followed the direction, but no lights.

'You are over the airfield,' came from the controller.

I performed another landing manoeuvre. As soon as we turned even slightly, the lights disappeared as if switched off abruptly. They must have lit some diesel; something was flickering in the dark.

I tried another approach.

Suddenly a row of lights popped on. We were flying across it. Another full throttle, back up and another landing manoeuvre, this time with flaps down.

'Watch your speed ... hangar opposite,' warned the controller.

We flew just above the ground again. I put the Wimpy on its wing and turned quickly before the lights disappeared once more. To fly the plane with flaps down took a lot of hard work.

At last I could see the landing lights from the right direction, but as we got closer, we were engulfed in fog again. But I had to risk it – we were low on fuel.

I pulled the joystick. Finally the wheels touched the ground from a height, jarring us violently. The plane bounced a few times.

We raced through the fog. I tried to keep the direction, breaking so hard that the tail was lifting with the ignition switched off. We stopped – at last. On one side a fire engine and few yards ahead of us the door of the hangar.

The Station Commander welcomed us wholeheartedly ...

As Ada Musalek had completed 200 operational hours he was posted as instructor, I became the captain and we got a new second pilot, Josef (Pepik) Filler. We were pleased. Rumour had it that he was a good omen for any crew. He was a cheerful stocky chap. If there was anything going on and the beer was flowing, Pepik was there too. Everybody liked him, the British as well.

He had only just got back from sick leave after injuring himself falling off a horse. Horses were the love of his life ... horses and people. Some claimed that horses would be his undoing one day, but he always laughed it off.

One evening while we were still living on the first floor of the farmhouse, we were woken by a commotion and voices. We recognized Pepik's voice.

'Come on, don't be frightened,' we heard from the stairwell.

'For God's sake, who is he bringing up here?'

'I hope it's not some woman!'

Judging by Pepik's gentle voice it could well have been a woman, but for the noise on the wooden steps. Somebody switched the light on.

Pepik's head appeared at the door, followed by a horse.

It took a lot of effort to get the frightened animal back down. We found out that a local lady farmer had lent it to Pepik so he wouldn't be late back ... and so he joined our crew.

When he had finished his 200 hours, he worked on the railways.

More ops: Nuremberg, Kiel, Hamburg, Berlin ...

We were given a week's holiday just before Christmas so we all went to London. Pavel took the opportunity to marry his Danish fiancée – a happy wedding, attended by the whole crew. Our traditional Czech Christmas Eve dinner in the new Mess was quite an occasion. The Wing Commander came too and, according to British tradition, served all the men.

The third year of the war was coming to an end ...

Chapter 9

Wilhelmshaven

The morning of 28 December, the first Sunday after Christmas.

Fog is slowly turning into rain and large drops falling onto the felt-covered roofs are the only disturbing sound of this otherwise quiet winter morning in the English countryside.

Nobody wants to get out of a warm bed in such weather. It's hard to imagine the front line and concentration camps in these circumstances. But war is still with us.

The fog thickens. Yesterday's ops were called off due to bad weather which was no better than today. Standby hasn't been called off yet today, but that usually happens at noon. A few forlorn figures appear out of the fog. We are slowly gathering for Sunday breakfast. The smell of fried bacon lifts our spirits. We all agree that ops will be called off again.

It's 1000 hrs and no sound of the roll call. Cyrda Sebela, from my old pre-war squadron, and I contemplate the best place for our afternoon trip. Cyrda pulls on his moustache and suggests Cambridge. He's heard there are plenty of pretty girls there.

At lunch everybody is feeling relaxed. No wonder, the weather is more suitable for a game of cards than a raid. Before everybody has managed to make plans for the afternoon off, the familiar voice from the speaker calls: 'Operation calling – attention please.' He continues mercilessly: 'All crews to operations room at 1400 hrs.'

The announcement puts a stop to all small talk.

The discussion resumes, without the cheerfulness. Everybody is guessing. Will we fly tonight? But mainly 'Where to?'

It's almost 1400 hrs and the ops room is filling up. Each crew takes its place at the large table, some of us looking over the known targets on the big map. Each has got its own memories – often not very pleasant ones. Perhaps it will be Bremen again? It was there when I saw Soukup's crew for the last time before their plane exploded in mid-air. The tension is palpable.

Our Squadron Commander sits behind his desk and keeps looking at us with a watchful eye. It is not easy for him. He is strict, strict but kind, and leads by example. What's he thinking about right now? Who is he seeing for the last time?

At 1400 hrs he begins. 'Quiet please.'

The silence is absolute. Everybody wants to know what's going to happen.

'The following crews have been selected for tonight's op ...' he continues, reading out the list of names and adds with each 'and his crew'. Any changes are announced separately. We've got a new second pilot, Josef Tomanek. We all call him Tom.

'Those whose names weren't read out, please leave the room.'

He doesn't have to say it twice. Only the more seasoned crews have been chosen. The weather is too bad for the less experienced ones.

When the last of them have left the room, the Operations Officer pulls back the curtain to reveal a large map on the wall. Everybody calms down again and the Squadron Commander continues, 'Tonight's target is Wilhelmshaven.'

The tension eases off a bit, though many release their feelings by coughing or shuffling their feet. The worst is over. The thin red string marking the route for tonight is really quite short.

'Chaps, this will be one of our shortest ops. And you, Pavel, will be back sooner than from the pub.' I try to reassure Pavel with a joke as it's just a week after his wedding.

'You will fly over the sea both ways. Your target is the docks. Approach from ...'

The Squadron Commander gives us a precise description of the target and the angle of approach based on the information about the least concentration of the German defences. The Intelligence Officer hands out the latest photographs of the target and gives us the whereabouts of known anti-aircraft guns, night fighters, balloons, searchlights and flak. Last of all he hands out small packets with foreign currencies and a map – just in case.

The navigator makes notes about the weather conditions: fog and drizzle over England, broken cloud over the North Sea, possible ice forming at 9,000 feet; over the target, clear and no wind.

The wireless operator notes the times, names and call numbers of the beacons that will be working that night. Together with the navigator they assess the distances of the marked points on the map, and count the timing and compass bearing for each part of the flight.

The Armaments Officer describes the type and amount of bombs carried.

The Squadron Commander takes over again. 'Take off at 18.15. Expect to reach the target at 21.15.'

He announces the starting order and finishes with the customary 'You know the rest – watch out. Good luck!'

We pack our gadgets. Not very cheerful now, but less morose than if we were going over to the Ruhr or deep into Germany. We leave the ops room.

It's getting dark outside; the fog feels even thicker. We bump into each other before our eyes adjust to it.

'Let's get ready.'

'Where the hell do they think they're sending us in this pea soup?'

We go and change into our warm underwear; we might need it tonight. It will be bloody cold up there and the heating usually stops at about 10,000 feet.

I always wear my little neck scarf on ops. It brings me luck. Many airmen believe in carrying a talisman and I am certainly one of them. I also take my toothbrush and toothpaste, so I don't have to come back after the meal.

The Mess is full and rowdy. One of our crews has just returned from hospital after landing in the sea back in September. I join them at their table. The pilot, Lenc, is describing how he was forced to ditch in the Irish Channel.

'I didn't think it would be such a hard landing. It's worse than a belly-landing on the ground. No, we didn't have to pump up the dinghy, it's automatic ... but, you know ... it still took some water in before we got there ... yes, they picked us up on the third day. But only two of us, the other four didn't make it.'

'Can't be helped, we're not sailors after all,' I butt in.

'True – water and us don't go together,' Lenc agrees.

We finish our high tea. It's time to go. Those staying behind tonight give us the thumbs up for good luck.

We always walk the short distance between the Mess and the airfield. Strange how precious those few hundred yards feel just before an op. I couldn't think of anybody who would have preferred to be driven. These are also the last few steps before donning our flying suits. Full winter kit including the Mae West and the parachute is very heavy indeed.

The messenger from the met office comes in with the update – no change tonight. Finally we each get a small packet of food.

Outside is the WAAF in uniform waiting to drive us to our plane. 'B please.'

I sit with her in the front and we move along the edge of the airfield. The fog and the darkness do not bother her; she knows the exact position of each plane by heart.

B for Bozena is waiting for us, looking very smart.

The head of the ground crew, now all Czechoslovaks, reports the plane ready and holds the ladder for us. Others pass the parachutes. We take up our positions and cross-check everything. I can see Pavel Svoboda turning the front turret and checking the movements of the machine guns. After the engine check I sign the logbook.

'Good luck, skipper.'

A group of mechanics are standing beside the left wing, thumbs up, earphones crackling.

'Control calling B for Bozena, get ready.'

'B for Bozena, understood.'

I switch over the intercom.

'How are we doing?'

'Navigator ready.'

Others confirm as well.

'Thank you. Gunners, leave the turrets. Ready to take off now.'

Back to the radio. 'B for Bozena, ready for take off now.'

'Control calling Bozena, take up your position behind the plane on your left, taking off third.'

'B for Bozena, understood.' I taxi close behind the tail light of the plane in front of us. The rest are invisible in the fog.

I turn the plane onto the grass take-off strip and spot the starter vehicle. I stop beside it, waiting for the green light. Shadowy figures move around the dimly lit vehicle. The strip must be lit up, but I can only see the first gooseneck. I try to position the plane correctly.

'Tom, flaps at fifteen.'

'Roger, fifteen degrees.'

The minute between the take-offs pass.

'B for Bozena, take off!'

'Green for us. Let's roll!'

I warn the crew and slowly pull the throttle. With brakes on I push the joystick to lift the fuselage and ease into the take-off run.

The engines roar and the tail eventually lifts. I ease off the brakes and we move.

It's slow. The plane is heavily loaded, the grass is wet and we are taking off slightly uphill. The second pilot is sitting beside me and watches the instrument panel. We pass the first gooseneck ... three others getting closer. The plane gathers speed. We need at least 90 miles per hour to get off the ground, which we must reach by the last gooseneck, otherwise we would not make it over the woods surrounding the airfield.

The engines still roar.

The plane sways and rocks on the uneven ground. The speedo reads ninety at last!

I peel the plane off the ground.

'Roger, undercarriage,' Tomanek confirms and pushes the lever. The undercarriage needs to be raised fast to reduce the air resistance and to avoid the risk of a crash while still flying low.

We climb gingerly. The plane hangs in the air. If one engine cuts off ... We perform the prescribed circuit over the airfield, gain height and set off on our flight course.

'Skipper, course zero seven five. What's our speed?'

'Roger, course zero seven five. Speed one two five.'

We are still in thick fog, cannot even see the wing tips. It's an uneasy feeling knowing how many planes are in the air at the same time – not just from our own airfield but from others as well. We all are tense and quiet.

We reach 3,000 feet and can start retracting the flaps, five degrees at a time. Even then the plane tends to nosedive and I have to adjust the elevator.

The fog disperses as we reach the cloud level.

We are near the Channel. The welcome change in the weather prompts everybody into action. With improving visibility we need to be on constant lookout.

The wireless operator and navigator check our direction. We are on course.

We are now flying alone, with no other planes in view, and below us it's pitch dark. Even the sound of the engines is different from when over land.

'Chaps, check your guns.'

A short blast follows, one from each turret. A vital check before any fighting starts.

We are not in any immediate danger so we take the chance to get some rest. The wireless operator tries to tune in to a Czech broadcast, but to no avail.

'Front gunner – flashes below right.'

'Josef, switch the radio off, we are getting close. It could be German flak ships.'

The first stars appear in the cloudless winter sky.

On our right we make out the snow-covered East Friesian Islands. Behind the last of them – Wangeroog – the snowy coastline along the Bay of Jutland turns southwards.

The flashes ahead increase and become more colourful. They're like fireworks, no doubt, but it means we're getting close to the target. Our undivided attention is needed.

Chapter 10

The Last Raid

Wilhelmshaven is not far away now.

'Lojzo, I'm homing in,' announces the navigator Pepa Mohr and takes up his position as the bomb-aimer at the front of the aircraft.

'Go through the middle of the bay and I will take you in.'

'Roger. Strange how little flak there is ...'

The tension is overwhelming. The navigator requests a slight change of course.

'Chaps, the Wimpy ahead of us just got caught by flak,' reports the front gunner.

I, too, can now see the Wellington amidst a high concentration of anti-aircraft fire. I take advantage of the situation and on half-throttle start descending towards the target.

We are losing height. Faint silhouettes of buildings become visible against the snow-covered ground. Seemingly the Germans have not noticed us yet. Or are they up to some trick?

'Skipper, course one eight five!'

'Roger, one eight five.'

'Hold it, speed one fifty!'

'Roger.'

The flares now illuminate the whole harbour.

'Bomb doors!'

'Bomb doors open, holding the horizon, speed one fifty.'

'Bombs gone!'

We feel a slight lift as each bomb leaves the plane. Six of them were dropped. After a while we hear Blondy Skalicky calling from the back, 'Target hit!'

The rear gunner is the only one who can see the action behind us and at some stage during a raid our safety depends entirely upon him.

'Lojzo, hold her, I'm taking pics!'

While the navigator takes the obligatory photographs as proof of us fulfilling our orders, the wireless operator reports back to England, 'KX-B dropped the bombs at 2040 hrs.'

The navigator comes in.

'Skipper, all done. Course zero zero and give it some stick so we can get out of here pronto!'

'OK, hold on to your hats everybody!'

The engine noise is deafening as we are flying on full throttle. Below us more and more fires appear, interspersed with tracer from the anti-aircraft batteries. Scores of flak bursts fill the sky. Some almost get us but luckily only cause us temporary blindness.

We manage to escape thanks to some neck-breaking manoeuvring.

I would never have believed how much a Wimpy can take and wouldn't dream of executing similar manoeuvres in daylight.

We are flying low and the visual tracers of the anti-aircraft fire are getting too close for comfort. They even come in different colours.

The plane shakes violently a few times.

'Shell bursts ahead on the port side,' reports Svoboda.

'Got them, Pavel. Going in!' I reply.

I bank the plane to the right into some puffs of smoke on the assumption that the anti-aircraft gunners won't aim twice at the same spot. I desynchronize the engines to make their aiming more difficult, and change our speed and height at the same time. This should get us over the sea as soon as possible. Both gunners take their turn in reporting new sightings of exploding shells.

It's not looking good.

Finally we leave the target and the land behind. I synchronize the revs and start climbing slowly.

'Everybody all right?'

The first reply comes from the rear turret, followed by the usual 'OK' from the rest of the crew.

'You gave us a hard time!'

'I did my best.'

I can unclip the belts now and hand the controls over to Josef Tomanek – Tom, my second pilot.

'Hold the course and keep climbing. I'll have a look at the back.'

I squeeze past the navigator and the wireless operator, and acknowledge their smiles with a thumbs up. We've got away with it once again.

From the astrolobe I can see not only the stars but also the whole top surface of the plane. No visible damage showing. The skies around us are still clear and peaceful. What a difference!

I am happy; the engines are purring. One more glance over the plane and I am on my way back.

Tom greets me with the eager smile of a new pilot. This is only his third operation and he is doing well. Like everybody before him, he was slightly nervous to start with, but he is settling in now.

Another strange vibration sweeps the plane.

I shine the torch on the control panel. Portside engine oil pressure gauge is jumping and then the needle starts falling.

'Tom, let me take over and go and start pumping oil!'

The pressure keeps on falling. I reduce the revs to help the engine. Uneven revs cause vibration.

A sharp rumble from the engine follows and first sparks appear. I quickly shut the fuel supply down.

'Tom, leave it and come back!'

Sparks are replaced by flames. Inside the plane it's all quiet. The crew obviously don't know anything yet. I am glad – panic is the last thing we need now. Tomanek is back and from the cockpit he spots the flames, just as Scerba calls, 'We are on fire!'

'I know. Don't worry, chaps. As soon as the fuel has burned out, I will douse it.'

I press the extinguisher button. The flames disappear and the engine is covered in white foam.

'All done! We'll have to fly on one engine only. Josef, report our position!'

The engine is shut down and flames extinguished, though the propeller is still spinning slowly by the force of the air pressure. A strange rumbling noise is coming out of the engine.

The starboard engine is working fully but we are still losing height. It is difficult to keep the plane in a straight line and we seem to be going round in uneven circles.

The navigator has got his hands full trying to follow our position on the map. Rightfully he asks, 'Lojziku, will we make it back to England?'

'Hopefully. But even if we land at sea, it would be close to the shore and they'd pick us up in the morning.'

'Hull confirmed our position and wants us to keep receiving,' Scerba reports.

'There you are. They know about us and will keep monitoring. Nothing to worry about ...'

Each minute is precious now. I find it hard work to hold the course as best I can. The main thing is not to lose any more height – it's dark and below us is the North Sea.

'Josef, any news from Hull?'

'Nothing. I'm listening in.'

A momentary silence is shattered by a sharp rumble which reverberates through the whole plane.

I can see the three-bladed propeller breaking up and falling out of the airframe, together with the engine. A heavy thump follows and the joystick is knocked out of my hand. The right engine's revs are falling. I try to accelerate but the joystick returns and the engine does not respond. It feels as if it's caught on something. We are losing speed.

'Gunners, leave your positions! Landing at sea!'

Silence follows.

The red warning light starts flashing. The front gunner can't open his turret. I grab Tomanek's shoulder and shout into his ear, 'Help Pavel!'

He must have misunderstood as he starts opening the floor exit door and puts his parachute on.

'What are you doing? We're above water!'

I scream at him and kick the door shut. He gets the message, takes the parachute off and moves towards the turret. Pavel is trying to get through but I stop him.

'Take care of the dinghy ropes.'

The dinghy is a rubber inflatable stored inside a small chamber in the right wing. On hitting the water surface it will be released automatically and inflate.

Pavel nods.

'Get ready!'

I pull Tomanek nearer to help me level the plane. All gauges are jammed and there is a strange whistling noise. We are falling through the clouds; I cannot judge our height. Eventually we manage to hold the flaps in position. I feel the plane going into a nosedive.

We drop out of the clouds into the darkness below. I don't even know the speed or the angle of our fall.

I must inflate the airbags. They will act as floats and can keep the plane floating for several hours ... so they say. But first I must ditch the bomb carriers. I start pressing the button but nothing happens. The hydraulics have packed up, the carriers will remain attached and the airbags will burst.

What if?

I keep pressing the button. Suddenly I spot a shiny black surface ... the sea. We are getting close. I scream.

'Hold on!'

I brace myself and pull on the controls to minimize the impact.

The wing touches the water surface and I black out ...

Chapter 11

Shipwrecked

In my dreams I hear a roar. It comes and goes. Then I feel the cold ... water ... I am coming slowly round. There is a sweet taste in my mouth. I am spitting blood as the next spray of icy water brings me round fully. My head is spinning. Slowly I begin to realize what has happened. My safety belt was not fastened and I hit my head on the crossbar.

The water splashes around me, rising and falling.

Water starts pouring in through the open cockpit above my head. The force of it knocks me down and drags me over but thankfully I am still attached to the oxygen supply through my flying helmet.

I undo the buckle and submerge in the freezing water. I manage to grab the edge of the wing and with the other hand punch a hole in the cover of the side near me to get a hold. I must be able to hold onto it somehow! The wreck is swaying. It is difficult to get out of the water in all that clothing. The waves are knocking me back.

Eventually I manage to climb onto the wing and the main body of the plane. I sit astride and catch my breath. I am soaked through.

By the tip of the right wing I spot something yellow – a dinghy. Our emergency rubber boat.

I shuffle along the fuselage. Somebody's head pops out of the astrolobe and disappears again. If only it was not so bloody dark! I lean inside and help somebody out. It is Scerba, his face covered in blood.

'Get into the dinghy!' I yell and point to the yellow object in water.

I am lying on the top and call inside, 'Anybody there?'

Nobody responds. I search around in the water with my hands. Nothing. The plane is partially submerged.

'We're here. Come over now or you'll go down with her!'

Somebody calls my name and I scramble into the dinghy head first. We are squashed in like sardines in a tin, unable to recognize each other. Someone is complaining that he cannot move and will drown. It sounds like Tomanek. His hands are entangled in the aerial, still attached to the aircraft. Somehow he manages to free himself.

We try to rearrange our seating positions and I call everybody by name.

'Blondy,' I repeat. Ruda Skalicky does not answer.

The only sound around is the sea. We look at the wrecked plane. The high tailpiece points out like some sort of memorial.

One part of the dinghy seems to be pulled downwards. I set to investigate only to find that we are still attached to the sinking aircraft. I kneel and feel for the release mechanism but to no avail. The situation is getting desperate. The thin cable could damage the dinghy. I wrap the cable around my hand and pull as hard as I can.

It works. The dinghy pops out but my fingers hurt badly. The flesh is cut right through.

We are free – but sad.

The wreck slowly sinks taking our friend with it.

'Poor Blondy, it's over for him. Whatever next?'

'He was next to me,' explains Pavel Svoboda. 'He must have been knocked unconscious and did not come round in time.'

Above us we can hear the other planes returning home.

We are sad, but the feeling's not the same as at a funeral. Possibly because Death is so near.

My watch has stopped at 2120 hrs.

'Listen everybody, we've got to seat ourselves properly.'

We find our voices again, as one by one we relate our own experiences while the others search for the emergency supplies. Everything is tied to the main rope. We find two bottles of drinking water, two small bottles of rum, two flares, a torch, two canvas oars, two tins of biscuits, various pills and, at last, an air pump. We make good use of the pump straight away.

'I was waiting for confirmation from Hull,' says Scerba holding his face, 'and suddenly there was this huge thump and the radio table collapsed. Something hit me in the face. I felt the blood running down my cheek. The light went out, the phone started crackling. I tried to get out of my seat. I met Pavel and Pepa in the fuselage and joined them. I had to prop myself as the plane was rocking. Somebody was shouting that we were landing in water. I pushed the button and my Mae West inflated. The next thump threw me to the floor. I hit myself hard and probably lost consciousness. When I came round, the plane was full of water. I tried to find my way out. I had to feel my way in complete darkness, trying to assess my position. I grabbed somebody's legs but they disappeared above my head. Then I saw a lighter spot – the opening of the astrolobe. After that Lojzek helped me out. What about you, Pavel?'

'I braced myself and held on firmly, expecting two thumps as usually happens when landing on water. The first one came all right but instead of the second one I got drenched. I tried to get out. Somebody's legs were hanging out of the astrolobe. I thought of getting out through the pilot's cabin. But when I opened the door, water came pouring out. I pushed the door shut and returned. The astrolobe exit was free. As I was climbing out, somebody else grabbed my legs ... was it you?'

'I bashed my knee badly,' complains Pepa Mohr. 'I was holding onto the astrolobe with one hand. After the crash landing I opened the hatch and climbed out. Jumping into the dinghy I got caught on the same aerial as Tom.'

'Pepa, by your reckoning, how far are we from the shore?' I interrupt the navigator's story.

'According to my last-known reading, about ninety miles from England.'

'They knew our position just before the crash, so our situation isn't too bad. We just have to wait until the morning.'

'They're probably still calling ...' I sum up for everybody.

The winds strengthen. We catch a glimpse of the stars through broken clouds. The roar of the sea intensifies. We can feel the waves rising.

We would have been back by now ...

The lucky ones who have made it back won't be sleeping either. They'll all be listening in to catch the sound of returning aircraft. The duty officer will be sitting by the telephone hoping to receive the news of our emergency landing elsewhere. But this time there is no point. Soon the HQ of No. 3 Group will announce officially that the crew of aircraft KX-B is missing ...

We can't see very far, only a few metres about us. The spray, which hits us from time to time, is white. The water level inside the dinghy is still rising; we need to scoop it out.

I empty one of the biscuit tins and it soon passes through everyone's hands. It's not easy. Water is gathering around our backs.

Our adrenalin drops as we begin to realize the enormity of our situation. We are shipwrecked. Our numbed senses start functioning properly. It is cold, we are soaked to the bone and sitting in water.

'Here it comes – I'm catching a cold,' Tomanek says and sneezes.

'A hot toddy will soon put it right.' Pepa Mohr tries to cheer him up. His humour is catching.

'I've had some strange sleeping arrangements in my time, but nothing this bad.' I can't even say that properly as my upper lip is swollen. We shuffle our legs around. Pavel sits next to me and complains that he has not got his boots.

'Where have you left them?'

'Somewhere in the plane.'

'You're not missing anything. Mine are full of water.'

We can hear planes passing overhead. Probably Stirlings on their way back from Germany. Somebody suggests firing a flare to catch their attention.

'There's no point in the dark. We'll need them tomorrow when they start looking for us ...'

We fall silent. Occasionally someone swears as he gets another cold shower. Our first night comes to an end and darkness slowly gives way to dawn. The wind keeps rising.

Sleep does not come. In my mind I am still going over the events before the crash ... did I do everything right? Yes, my belt was not fastened ... that was a mistake. Only now do I begin to feel fear. There was no time for it before.

I shiver all over. Is it the cold?

I am back in my flat in Otrokovice the night before my escape. I could not sleep that Sunday night either. Eman's last instructions are flooding back: 'Don't forget the flaps ... keep her close to the ground ... you have got enough fuel to get to Zagreb ... don't worry, the Germans won't have time to fire at you ... here is your pistol ... be careful...'

I open my eyes suddenly and look at the others. Their heads are down, seemingly asleep.

My eyes are closing again. I am back home, again preparing to fly out with the Zlin Z-XIII prototype next morning ...

75

Our bodies shiver even more as freezing water washes over us. Somebody is shouting. Eman? No, not Eman Krejci, he never shouted. It's Pavel ... he must have been dreaming. It's quiet now and I am back home once more. This time in Ostrava with Kocfelda and Valasek. When we tried to escape the first time, it was also a horrible night. Those two made it to Poland and I felt the same shiver as I had to turn back.

All that suspicion and constant fear – I was cold then ...

I'm cold now ...

The joy of the dawn light is replaced by disappointment. The horror we could only feel in the dark, we can now see. Huge walls of water are rolling towards us ready to squash us. Waves glide underneath, lifting us on their crests, which break over our heads. We will turn over! One wave leaves us with a crash, we are falling and another is upon us. We are a mere toy for the elements. We can't see the horizon as the gunmetal grey of the sea merges with the December sky.

We feel seasick. One bout after another. As if our insides are being torn out.

The dinghy is filling up again as bailing out becomes ever more difficult. It starts to deflate so we try to pump it up. Pavel is kneeling over the edge of the dinghy. When it is his turn to bail out the water, I pass him the tin. He does not take it, just kneels there silently.

On my right Tomanek is crying. 'If only I had a pistol ...'

'Tom, hold on. We're strong blokes after all!'

'Of course we'll get through. They'll find us. You'll see.' Mohr butts in.

Scerba on the other side just listens but his big eyes don't seem to register what's going on. He doesn't speak, only stares ahead.

The sea shows its cruelty to the full. It rises as if it wants to drag us down to the bottom. The icy wind tears at our faces. We cannot hear anything but the roar of the waves and howling of the wind. All eyes are still searching for the rescue craft. Suddenly Tomanek shouts, 'Sub! Ship!'

But there is nothing ... just the vast expanse of rising waves.

The dinghy is round and keeps turning and bobbing. Another huge wave disappears underneath our meagre craft and we plunge down between the next two. Back up again and our horizon broadens briefly.

'Look!' Scerba calls, his eyes focussing somewhere behind me. I turn round. A mere 3 metres from us is a mine. Some rescue this is turning out to be ...

Its detonators stick out horribly. We grab the two canvas oars and paddle as fast as we can ... the rest paddle with their bare hands ... away, away from it. It feels as if we're going nowhere. Luckily the current carries us faster but even so we only just miss the mine. Tomanek's sub, our prospective rescuer, disappears. We are glad but disappointed at the same time.

Our first day is almost over. 29 December 1941 has ended.

Chapter 12

Lost Hope

Depression weighs us down.

It's getting dark again. With the deepening gloom the wind eases off; even the sea seems calmer. The waves disappear into the abyss, only the rough black surface remains. What a relief! We scoop more water out and pump up the dinghy. Nobody needs to be asked, we are in better spirits and the hope of rescue grows stronger again.

The narrow shape of the moon is visible through the thinning clouds.

'Why don't we try to paddle towards the West?' suggests Mohr. 'We can navigate by the moon. At least we could get nearer our last known location at the time of the crash.'

We get on with it instantly but it's easier said then done. The round shape of our dinghy hampers our efforts and we keep turning round. We have to paddle in pairs, against each other, with the navigator monitoring our course. We take it in turns until we drop with exhaustion.

We spend the best part of the night hoping for rescue and forgetting the reality. That appears to be the only positive outcome of all our efforts. Those few hundred yards would hardly make any difference.

We stop paddling. It's quiet and the sea surface glistens. Again we can hear the engines of aircraft returning from Germany. How many did not make it this time?

The moon disappears as the dawn arrives. With the increasing light the wind strengthens again. We are exhausted after the second sleepless night. The sea gets up again, the waves small at first, but soon reaching their enormous proportions.

Scerba and Tomanek have still got their flying helmets; the rest of us are bareheaded, our hair matted with salt. We are still sitting in water and our legs, resting on each other's, don't seem to belong to us any more.

The monotonous roar of the sea is broken only by the occasional splash of spray, which merely adds another few gallons of water to the dinghy.

We don't talk, our heads resting on our chests. We can't sleep for pain and cold. We are too exhausted. We just wait and wait.

It's now broad daylight again and the sky has regained its monotonous shade of December grey. Somebody tries to lift his legs. Pepa complains about his knee. They all need encouragement.

'Come on you lot! We must get that water out! Where's the tin? Somebody pump up that dinghy, it's getting low again!'

They look absent-minded. It takes a while before one of them reacts. Tomanek tries to move and moans immediately. Pavel takes care of him.

'Let me have a look at that hand of yours. It'll hurt like mad at first. Lojzku, grab his hand tight!'

He gathers his broken fingers, straightens them and uses the tin lid as a splint. It helps. Tomanek does not moan so much now.

The sea rages on but the seasickness does not bother us much any more – we must be getting used to it. If only we were not so thirsty. Somebody screams 'Thirst' and we all are consumed by the desire to quench it. One of us opens the small bottle of rum; others struggle with the top of the water bottle. The rum ration amounts to only a sip, but there simply is not enough water. Even two litres in one go would not be sufficient now.

'How about sea water?'

'Yuck – I don't like it even inside my boots,' I shudder.

Too late. The first one picks up the tin. Pavel tries to warn Tomanek.

'Don't swallow it. It's said to be very harmful. Just gargle and spit it out!'

We keep watching each other to see whether everybody spits it out. I reprimand Scerba, 'Josefe, you are swallowing it, I can see it.'

'Just one little sip . . .' he argues and anxiously awaits its impact. It is hard, really hard to spit it out. Our thirst is overwhelming.

Our stomachs are now cleaned out by sea water. My suggestion to eat some biscuits is welcomed by all. If only it was that easy. I find it impossible to swallow even a small piece without the help of water.

'They must have baked these to last not to be eaten.' I give up.

And so it goes on. A piece of biscuit and a sip of sea water. There is no other way. After all, we have not eaten for forty-eight hours.

Is it lunchtime or dinner? Hard to judge. The severity of the weather and none of our watches working allow only a wild guess. We can only count the days and nights ...

Today is 30 December. The second night has passed and the second day of hoping and waiting is upon us.

The sea spray mercilessly lashes at our ashen faces. My cut fingers are badly swollen.

The cuts look horrible but they neither hurt nor sting any more. I feel a strange tingling in my feet as if my boots are too small. I ask Pavel to help me take them off. It is not easy as my feet are so swollen.

I try to use one of my boots to scoop the water out. It doesn't work as I don't have enough space. So I toss both boots into the sea.

'You know what? I feel better without them!'

Others soon follow my example.

Time passes so slowly!

The sea wallows. We are alone with our thoughts. Suddenly I hear a faint humming. Or is it just a dream?

With baited breath I listen. The humming grows louder. I look at the others. They too slowly open their eyes. With our mouths open we try to catch the sound. What if it stops?

The humming gets nearer ... yes ... there's no mistake ... an aircraft engine! We are very lively now and scream in unison, 'Aircraft!'

But we can't see anything. Our eyes scan the winter sky. Mohr starts pointing forward and shouts, 'There it is!'

We can all see it now. There are two of them, flying too high for us to be sure they are ours or German.

One of the planes turns. Soon it is above our heads. It's ours! We shout and whistle as best as we can, not even realizing they can't hear us anyway. The plane passes us by at 300 metres.

'Flares!'

Mohr nervously tries to set one off. Too bad, it fails and the plane flies on.

'Give me the other one!' I scream and snatch it from Mohr's hand. I shove the handle into Pavel's hand and release the catch. Everybody's eyes follow my every move. The plane is disappearing and this flare is our last and only hope of rescue. The sea tosses us around.

I pull the catch. The flare hisses, the first charge passing my head.

'Let go!' I take the flare from Pavel and aim at the departing plane. Somebody else counts the charges. There should be thirteen of them. Six gone and they still have not spotted us. We're seriously worried.

'Eleven.' Suddenly there is a flash from the plane. They have seen us and fire their flare. The plane is coming back. A wave knocks the flare out of my hand, the last charge falls into the water.

It doesn't matter. The aircraft flies past, turns again and comes even nearer. We wave and they wave back. It is a Hudson from Coastal Command. While the plane circles overhead, the dinghy is alive. We all gulp, our hearts in our throats.

'Looking forward to New Year's Eve!' shouts Mohr happily.

'Hmm, I don't think I'll manage any decent dancing on my legs.' I pinch my swollen limbs and add, 'I'll soak them in a bucket of drinking water and my throat with something else.'

Pavel is looking forward to seeing his young wife.

The plane is back. Something falls from it. Yes, it's a package for us. We know there will be some water, clothing and food. We grab the oars and paddle for life. It's impossible. The sea is very rough and soon we start losing sight of it.

'I'll swim after it,' suggests Tomanek. Hardly – he too finds that he has no feeling in his legs. We keep paddling; the dinghy turns and heaves. The package eventually disappears altogether. We are exhausted but in high spirits. Our rescuer is still flying nearby; we will be fine.

'Pity about the package. Never mind, they'll get us out soon!'

The plane continues to circle.

'He must be giving our position to the nearest craft, so they can come and fish us out!'

'We shall invite them to celebrate with us.'

'I'll offer all my pay!'

'Me too ... me too ...'

Pavel adds up. It'll be some party, he reckons.

'I'll bring my wife too!'

One suggestion follows another, our eyes firmly fixed on the plane. The Hudson does another circuit, tips her wings and departs slowly. We can hardly keep our eyes open. They hurt so much as we try not to lose sight of her. The sound of the engines weaken. We can't see the plane any more.

It's getting dark. Our hopes are high and we keep cheering each other up.

'They know our position. They'll pick us up in the morning, you'll see!'

'It's never failed before!'

'We'll hold on until the morning but we must stop drinking that water!'

We grow quiet. Darkness falls, our constant companion. We've had a very exciting and exhausting day which has ended in disappointment.

We are resting now, our heads bowed. The dinghy is quiet; only the sea carries on regardless. Five men up to their waists in water, frozen to the bone. There is no point bailing out the water any more ... as much as it's pointless to try and quench our thirst.

The water is really cold. We are, after all, in the North Sea on 30 December.

What about my legs ... or are they somebody else's? It doesn't matter – they all look the same, swollen and blue. I pinch mine but can't feel a thing.

The night is approaching but the wind doesn't ease off. The moon is covered in clouds. My eyes are closing, but sleep doesn't come, only weird visions.

I can see tables covered in white cloth and laden with drinks, but I can't reach ... that thirst again!

It's torture. I try to push my eyes open with my senseless fingers just to get rid of this vision. I even try to talk to the others. The thirst is stronger. We all give in and help ourselves to more sea water. It is not salty or bitter any more, just cold.

The third night passes. It's New Year's Eve. We wonder whether darkness is better for us than daylight? We all agree – daylight. We can at least manage to keep our eyes open and stop the horrible visions.

At dawn somebody spots a seagull. Yes, one lands nearby.

Five new pilots pass their final test at Bata Airfield, Otrokovice, 29 September 1936. The author is first from the right.
(Author's private collection)

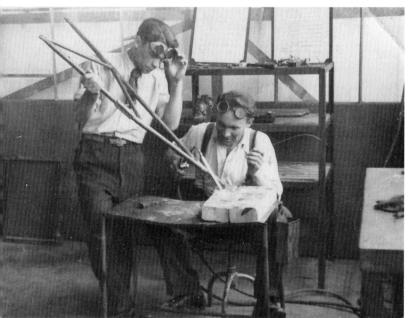

Author (standing) with the chief welder Mr Rocek during the work on Zlin XII plane project.
(Author's private collection)

As an additional qualification author (centre) also became a driving instructor.
(Author's private collection)

New recruits outside Vyskov barracks (author third from the right). (*Author's private collection*)

Author with Ruda Havlicek in front of aircraft type S-16-28 of 2nd wing, Olomouc airfield 1937. (*Author's private collection*)

National service. First leave (from the left) Frantisek Seda, author, Vitek. (*Author's private collection*)

In the shadow of an A-100. *(Author's private collection)*

The Citadel, Budapest. *(Author's private collection)*

With the inmates of the Citadel (the author is hiding at the back row in the centre of the photograph), spring 1940. *(Author's private collection)*

Roll call at Agde French Foreign Legion Camp. *(Author's private collection)*

Arriving at Falmouth on 24 June 1940. *(Author's private collection)*

The author (centre) with A. Pospichal and S. Linka during their first leave after swearing allegiance to the King. *(Author's private collection)*

Refuelling a Wellington of 149 Squadron. (*Author's private collection*)

Crews on the way to their Wellingtons (149 Squadron). (*Author's private collection*)

Wellington pilots in the cockpit. (*Author's private collection*)

Dinghy training. *(Author's private collection)*

KX-M after belly landing having been attacked over the airfield on return from a bombing raid over Hannover. *(Author's private collection)*

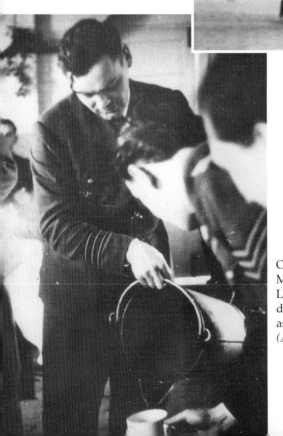

Opening of the new Sergeants' Mess, 28 October 1941. Squadron Leader Josef Ocelka serves the drinks which the author distributes as the head of the Mess. *(Author's private collection)*

The author in 1941.
(*Author's private collection*)

After a direct hit there was
no chance of escaping.
(*Author's private collection*)

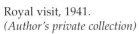

Royal visit, 1941.
(*Author's private collection*)

KX-B en route to Wilhemshaven on 28 December 1941. (*Author's private collection*)

A last farewell to those who did not make it. (*Author's private collection*)

KX-M in formation. (*Author's private collection*)

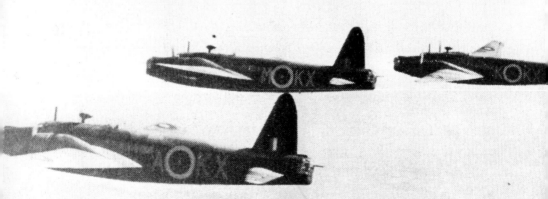

KX-M on her own. *(Author's private collection)*

Dutch coast near
Bergen am Zee.
*(Author's private
collection)*

Gestapo archive picture
of the author, Stalag
IXC, Obermansfeld.
(Author's private collection)

Inmates at Obermansfeld (the author is in the back row, third from the right). *(Author's private collection)*

Colditz Castle. *(Author's private collection)*

Czechoslovak inmates in Colditz. The gap fourth from the right was left for the author who was too sick to attend. *(Author's private collection)*

The author (left) as a liaison officer after the liberation.
(*Author's private collection*)

Outside the gates of the Queen Victoria Hospital, East Grinstead.
(*Author's private collection*)

The author giving evidence at the Globke war crimes trial, Berlin 1963.
(*Author's private collection*)

The author with wife
Vlasta, Kolin, 1968.
(Author's private collection)

The author (second from
right) with other Colditz
inmates, Pat Reid and
Kenneth Lockwood, in
Cambridge, 1987.
(Author's private collection)

Thomas Zuiderland at
Mohr's grave in Bergen.
(Author's private collection)

The Queen and Duke of Edinburgh's visit to Prague in 1996. They are accompanied by President Vaclav Havel. *(Author's private collection)*

With HRH Prince Charles during his visit to Prague in 2000 *(photo courtesy of the Czech Press Agency)*.

Meeting Tomas Bata at the Czechoslovak Military Ball in March 2000. (*Author's private collection*)

With fellow Guinea Pigs during their visit to Prague. (*Author's private collection*)

The author with his squadron.
(*Author's private collection*)

Returning to Colditz in August 2003. The author is on the right with fellow ex-inmate, Petr Uruba.
(*Author's private collection*)

The author's last official
photograph.
(*Author's private collection*)

Order of the White Lion III.
Category (Military Group)
(*Author's private collection*)

'We can't be too far away from the shore.'

'They'll find us!'

We try to reassure ourselves. No need for a rota to bail the water out now. Everybody tries his best. We will survive!

It's amazing how one seagull can capture the attention of five men in our situation. The sea is rough but the seagull doesn't seem to mind. The waves bring him within arm's length. We are very quiet and rigid with fear that any sudden move could frighten him away. Our new hope!

Rescue doesn't come but the seagull stays. The excitement is overridden by tiredness. And the thirst is back.

'What if we caught it?'

'That would be lovely!'

'The blood would revive us.'

'The flesh wouldn't be bad either.'

We calmly divide each drop of blood and each morsel of flesh while the seagull floats near us. It's near and yet too far for us to catch it. When it realizes that there's nothing to pick up, it takes off and disappears as fast as it came.

We're alone once again.

The day grows stronger and so does the wind. The sea rises and lashes at us without mercy. There is no point in ducking any more, we are too wet anyway.

From the stubble-covered faces stare sunken eyes. Blue lips move gently, some begging, some comforting, some damning. What hope have we got left? Will rescue come?

We have to occupy ourselves to stave off the worst. I open a small packet and lower it into the water on a piece of string. It leaves a fluorescent trail, which grows bigger behind us. It remains visible for several hours.

'It will help them to find us.'

Yesterday's disappointment is hard to describe. We cannot explain the fact that they have failed to pick us up. We all know only too well the unwritten rule of the Air Force: no one leaves a shipwrecked crew before summoning help. Why did the plane leave? Was it short of fuel?

Leaden clouds race across the sky above; further away they meet the sea. Occasionally we catch a glimpse of a watery winter sun.

It must be about midday. Perhaps. Who knows? It doesn't matter any more. Our lunch won't get cold.

We still try to make out any different sound in the cacophony of the sea. Our eyes scan the waves as far as they can. Nothing. We are just a pawn in the element's great game.

The green trace behind us is still visible. That surely must be the marker that will bring them to us.

Surely? What is certain now? Will they continue to search for us?

I feel my legs. The left one is somewhere at the bottom and the right one entangled with the others. No point pulling them together, they are all submerged.

And those faces . . .

Is that really Scerba opposite me?

I keep wondering whether I look as bad myself. I touch my swollen face; my fingers can't even feel the stubble.

It's getting dark again.

Nobody talks about hunger as we don't feel any. But our thirst is unbearable. It's persistent, but less demanding, and our visions grow simpler. Instead of opulent cafes and restaurants we see dirty knives, broken glasses on the tables and a few unfinished drinks. Doesn't matter who left them. If only I could reach those few drops of liquid before they soak into the floor.

Chapter 13

Happy New Year, 1942

The last night of the year approaches. The last day of our lives?

Yesterday and even this morning, we were still looking forward, perhaps rightfully so, to celebrating it with our friends.

Bitter thoughts are disrupted by Scerba's shouting. 'I can hear a ship!'

It takes a while now before any of us react. With gaping mouths we try to listen, peering into the darkness. Nothing, only our darkened silhouettes. Silence falls again. We grow suspicious that he's started hallucinating.

'I can see them ... there are three of them,' Pavel screams and points into the darkness.

We could not possibly see them at the same time – we are sitting in a circle and the movement of the sea does not help. What one can see, another one simply cannot.

Simultaneously we all start shouting and whistling just to get their attention.

'We need some light!'

Good idea, but how to do it? We have used up our flares and the torch packed up long ago. Tomanek's matches are too damp. We don't even care whether the ships are ours or German.

'I've got a lighter!' Pavel announces as a tiny spark appears.

'Hold on, if we lit something up, that would help!'

I stall his effort and pull a fiver out of my pocket. It's quite thin and large enough to produce some flame.

I hold it while Pavel repeatedly tries his lighter. And swears. All in vain, there is not enough fuel in it to light the paper. We despair ...

No one claims any more sightings of ships, although we can still hear a faint ticking of their diesel engines. Or is it our hearts beating so fast?

We stop talking. Nobody can sleep. It is obvious that we will miss tonight's festivities. Too painful to even talk about it.

The stars shine brightly and it's getting colder. The spray freezes in our hair, our eyebrows and on the collars of our flying jackets. I've even got small icicles on my pullover which crackle with every move. My mind is muddled up with all that excitement and disappointment. Somewhere the clock has probably struck midnight.

The New Year is upon us. We must believe it will bring rescue. I try to drum up everybody's spirits.

But that voice? It can't be mine!

Nobody responds. But I know they heard me, they are not asleep. Mohr doesn't join me any more. That's too bad. Tomanek groans.

Time passes. My eyes close. I can see the flak, hear the aircraft engines and shell explosions. From time to time one of us moves, shouts something and waves about.

Hallucinations, bad sign.

If only that thirst wasn't so bad. As soon as one takes a sip, more have to follow. After all, it probably doesn't matter any more.

Our strength is draining away ...

Dawn on New Year's Day mercilessly exposes our misery. After four nights we look dreadful.

Everywhere else people are opening new diaries and hope for a better future. Meanwhile, five human wrecks, with their ice-covered heads hanging down, fight the uneven battle for survival. Far away from the rest of the world we are our own spectators and judges. Who will go first – who will be last? Our chances are even.

Huge clumps of sea fog roll about. We can't see very far. Only the sea roars. We feel utterly hopeless.

Did somebody speak or was it just a groan?

Eyes open slowly and look around. What a sight! Drawn faces, sunken eyes, hair and beards caked in ice. Only through remembering our seating positions can we now recognize each other.

'Chaps, it's New Year's Day! Hold on, they must come and get us today!'

I can hardly say the words.

What should we wish each other? All the best? We wish each other rescue. It's more of a promise as we try to shake hands. Our swollen, blue and horrible-looking hands.

'We must paddle so we can get nearer England. There we will have a chance of being spotted by a ship or a plane ... Tom ... Pepiku ... Pavle ... do you hear me?'

I know paddling is pointless but some exercise would get them out of their growing lethargy. I have never needed to use the voice of authority within my crew before. We have always understood each other. That makes it more difficult now, looking at their devastated faces. It takes time before my words receive any reaction. We take it in turns. While some paddle, others try to spread their flying jackets to create some sort of a sail. We don't even know whether we're moving.

'Stop paddling!'

I lower a piece of weighted string into the water. It slowly sinks vertically.

'Start again!'

I watch as the string eventually rises to the surface.

'We're moving!'

My joy is brought about by the mere fact that we are still alive and doing something. It's unbelievable how much strength we can still find. Those who stop immediately quench their thirst. It's hard to tell how far we have actually progressed. But we certainly keep stopping more often and eventually we stop altogether. We can't navigate any more. A weak sun disappears behind the clouds.

Our first day of the New Year comes to an end. With the growing darkness our hopes fade. Night falls, tired eyes close but sleep does not come. Only the hallucinations return, dreams of the inevitable roller coaster of hope and hopelessness.

We grow impassive. We think we are asleep, but our weakened senses still register our surroundings, though our reactions are painfully slow.

I am back at home. Little sketches of my life keep coming back ... somebody shouts ... as a little boy walking to the church with my mother ... the path of the crosses ... music is playing, somebody sings ... kneels ... roses and blossoms ... I run down the hill and stumble ... my knee hurts ...

Another scream. Was it me?

Tomanek is leaning on me and tries to say something, but I can't understand a word. His legs jerk. The wind subsides. The moon is covered by a thin veil of cloud, our silent companion. The cloud thickens, the moon disappears. It does not feel so cold.

At dawn it starts drizzling. Our ashen faces reflect the pain and suffering of the last few days. Small droplets of water appear on my matted hair and even on the edge of my scarf wrapped around my forehead.

It provokes more thirst. I lick it once, twice and taste its sweetness. I pull the end of my scarf and lick it all over. It feels refreshing.

'Chaps ... it's raining!'

I wake the others.

'Lick the dew ... it's refreshing!'

They look around and wonder what I am up to. It's not really raining, just a slight drizzle. Soon we all lick our collars, sleeves and some even turn their flying jackets inside out and lick the fur. I can't do that. I've only got my battledress on. If only it would rain properly!

The wind grows stronger, clouds pass by faster and the drizzle stops. The sea opens up its game again. With no more drizzle, sea water is back on the menu.

We are gaining water but nobody attempts to bail it out. We can't pump up the dinghy either as the pump packed up long ago. Sea water saw to that too.

Pepa Mohr complains about a headache. He, too, has lost his flying helmet.

'Here, wrap this around your forehead.' I pass him my little scarf. It has lived around my neck, my talisman for good luck.

The wind picks up speed. The waves tower over us, spray beating our emaciated bodies. We are wet and deeper in the water than ever before.

It starts freezing. Nobody attempts to paddle, all strength gone. Given the swell it would be pointless anyway. Worse, it would drain whatever limited strength we still have left. And our thirst would increase. Depression follows.

'It's too late ... they'll never find us,' Tomanek moans.

'There's still some hope! We must hold on!'

Mohr suddenly joins me in my plea. He pulls out a photograph of his girlfriend and says – no, shouts – as if he wants her to hear it too, 'Evicka is with us, there is still hope!'

He breaks into a whisper which we can't follow.

Only Scerba is quiet, his dark eyes widely open, staring into oblivion. His lips are moving – is he praying?

It's getting dark again. The day feels somewhat shorter, due to the weather perhaps. All those low black clouds. Night falls quickly.

Our heads bow, lower than yesterday. Silence befalls the dinghy ...

I wake up. On my right Tomanek is breathing heavily, mumbling and swaying. Suddenly he shouts, 'Rabbit! Rabbit! Catch it!'

That's too bad. He's probably got a fever. He calms down. Darkness, silence and deep exhaustion overcome me. I lapse into semiconsciousness once more. In my dreams I see two huge lumps of black coal crushing the straw. I am that straw. I feel utterly hopeless, desperately trying to wake up. Tomanek moans again; I try to calm him down. He does not react, only trembles.

I worry he will fall into the water. I ask Pavel to help me tie him down. It is unbelievably difficult, our hands have lost all feeling and the sea tosses us around like a cork. And it's so dark.

'Rabbit ... rabbit!' Tomanek shouts repeatedly.

Suddenly Mohr, who is sitting opposite him, joins in. 'I can see it. I'll get it!'

From then on they chase after their rabbit, oblivious to our attempts to stop them. Their shouts are replaced by moans. They stop shouting and only whisper, 'Evicko! Mother ... mother!'

'Tom, you must hold on. Do you hear me?'

Tomanek does not respond. He opens his mouth but can't speak. Then he starts foaming at the mouth. His breathing changes into a groan. His head drops on my shoulder. I can hear his elaborate breathing for a little longer. Then it stops. His heavy body leans against me. I fight with the black lumps again ...

'Pavel, Tom is ...'

Pavel reaches for Tomanek's hand and checks his eyes.

'You are right.... '

I stammer but can't cry. Am I praying? I don't even know. I can't quite grasp the new reality – airmen don't die this way ...

My head is empty of any thoughts. Death was here, perhaps still is … I look around slowly. It might not be so bad. I don't feel any fear, just profound sadness. I can't see Death. The white in the distance is the ever-present sea spray.

I don't hear the bells toll, only the cacophony of the wailing wind and rising sea.

The dinghy is even quieter now; only Mohr breathes heavily. His head drops nearer the water surface. I turn to Scerba who is sitting next to him.

'Josef, hold his head or he will drown.'

I have to repeat my request. Even then it takes a while before Scerba reacts to it. Mohr's breath is now intermittent. He starts groaning, occasionally trying to say something. Scerba holds his head in silence.

'Pepiku … chin up! We must hold on. They will get us out!'

I keep calling him as Pavel tries to comfort him. It does not work. He was so optimistic only a short while ago.

Pavel and I discuss the situation. Tom is dead; Mohr is on his way out. Scerba's silent melancholy is also a cause for concern. We are filling up with water – it's up to our waists now. Pavel helps to straighten Tomanek's lifeless body.

Suddenly the silence increases.

Mohr has gone.

His head falls on Scerba's shoulder. Pavel and I try to pray, our hands unable to clasp together.

Something inside me protests. Sadness, hopelessness – anger? I don't really know. One thing is certain though. We are separated from the rest of the world, but perhaps closer to reality than others would be.

They were both our good and brave friends.

'How is Scerba?'

Pavel checks him, shouts at him, but Scerba does not respond. He is deeply unconscious.

How long will it take before we are all dead?

The waiting is the worst part of it. Who will be next? It will be worst for the last man alive. I am deep in thought, silently watching Pavel Svoboda. Will it be him or me?

Pavel's expression reveals the same thought.

Chapter 14

We Fight Death

'Lojzku, how long can we hold on?'

'Perhaps one more day.'

'You don't believe in rescue any more?'

'I was hopeful until yesterday.'

'Let's have a drink ... bloody thirst!'

I raise the tin to my swollen lips and curse the sea water.

'You bastard! You've already killed three of my friends and now you're waiting for us too!'

The water does not taste of anything any more; our burnt throats have lost all feeling. The sea rages; the dinghy is tossed about helplessly. We huddle together.

'I was never afraid of dying, Pavel. That was to be expected on every flight, especially during the war. But this! Blondy came off better then Tomanek and Mohr. One knock on the head finished him, no pain and suffering. I would not mind going the same way. But dying slowly while conscious – that's no way to go for a soldier.'

Scerba does not even stir.

'Pavle – I've got an idea – we could finish it ourselves ...'

'I know Lojzku. But we haven't got any pistols.'

'But we've got something else. In that tin are some drugs. If we took the whole lot, it might send us to sleep. Let Death come and get us then ... what a disappointment it would be if we cheated her! She's had her share already.'

Pavel agrees. It takes a lot of effort to open the wretched tin with our hands, but it's worth it. Pavel fills the tin with water and prepares the cocktail. I don't know whether he is thinking about anything. I am not. I am only worried that we will spill some of it. His hands are shaking.

'So, half and half ...'

Pavel drinks his half and hands over the tin. I finish it off.

'Mates for ever!'

We huddle and touch each other for the last time. All that's left is the waiting ...

I sense a strange buzzing inside my head; my eyes are heavier then ever. I want to sleep so much.

It's getting dark all around.... .

All of a sudden I hear a distant noise of flying birds. I don't feel any pain, in fact, I feel just fine. I don't know where I am nor do I sense anything. Strange silence, all seems beautiful. Have I died yet or am I on my way out? The buzzing comes and goes. I don't want to open my eyes. Have I moved?

'Lojzku, how are you?'

I hear a husky voice, then silence again. I can't understand what's going on; I just feel as if I am falling. The buzzing grows and grows until it becomes familiar. I begin to grasp the situation.

'Pavle, are you asleep?'

'No ... but I feel fine.'

'So do I. Didn't we die?'

I want to sing, but my throat is too dry. And the thirst is back.

Were we asleep, unconscious or just in a void? I am not able to answer that.

The dinghy is tossed about, the spray batters us, I feel faint ...

When I come round and eventually open my eyes, it's getting light. For the sixth time. It should be Saturday, 3 January.

The picture in front of me brings me sharply back to reality. The dinghy is full of water; only the yellow rim is still visible. We are sitting waist deep in water, Tomanek's stiff corpse towering over me. Mohr's bowed head is resting on Scerba's shoulder and Scerba's eyes are showing white.

Pavel's head is on my shoulder, propping my own swollen and unshaven face.

The empty tin is still in my hand ...

'What are we going to do?'

'Let's drown,' Pavel suggests.

'No way, I'd rather freeze to death ... Pavle, this must be a good omen. If we did not die now, we might be saved yet. But we must do something to hold on. The dinghy is sinking and we have no means of pumping it up.' I look around and Pavel gets the message.

'I know what you are thinking … we have to bury them …'

'Yes, we could lighten the dinghy, otherwise we'll all drown.'

I fasten Tomanek's flying helmet under his chin. Pavel tries to find his legs. Together we heave his stiff body over the edge. It takes a hell of a long time as the dinghy is too full and soft. Exhausted we pause for a while and then carry on. It's useless.

'I can't do any more. My legs have gone. Wake Scerba up. Maybe he is still alive and could help …'

'Wake up!' Pavel yells at him.

At last Scerba opens his eyes. His look is blank; he does not understand what's going on.

'Josefe, help Pavlovi,' I ask.

'We are burying Tomanek,' Pavel explains.

From Scerba's expression it is obvious that he has no idea about the two dead. With a sudden notion he grabs Mohr's head and presses it to his chest. I shout at him:

'Josefe, can you hear me? Help us. Mohr and Tomanek are dead. We are still alive and we must save ourselves!'

In the meantime Pavel manages to kneel and Scerba mechanically helps to throw Tomanek's body overboard. He's got a strange expression on his face. Progress is slow; my lifeless legs are in the way.

At last Tomanek's huge body slips over the edge of the dinghy and slowly sinks. A few bubbles … and it's over.

'Give our regards to Blondy,' I whisper and feel awful. Pavel and I pray for their souls.

Tom's place looks strangely vacant and we feel abandoned. Even dead, he was still with us.

The sea took away more than a corpse. We feel dull and our minds are completely blank. We are not capable of grasping anything, we can't even acknowledge each other. Perhaps it was that strange funeral without a grave or flowers. Not even the bells toll … only the sea rages on and the waves wash over us.

Cold water brings us back to reality once more. We became undertakers to save the living.

Mohr lies opposite. Pavel judges the situation but he cannot do it on his own.

'I can't get over to you. Josef must help you.'

Scerba's eyes are shut, his head bowed again and Pavel's efforts to wake him up don't work. Scerba is unconscious. Pavel tries on his own but it proves too much for him. He collapses totally exhausted. The thirst is back.

The wind howls, the sea rises and black clouds cover the skies. Further away they seem to fall into the water. Our heads are spinning and stomachs churning.

It's as though the sea has frozen and the clouds are racing by.

The situation in the dinghy is critical. Scerba has collapsed and his face is half in water.

'Pavle ... we have to sort this out. Let's sit him on Mohr's lap, otherwise he'll drown.'

'We must fasten him or he'll fall again.'

'OK, at least he'll cover Mohr's face. I can't bear looking at him any longer ... or I'll go mad!'

We fall silent. The half alive are joined with the dead, the half alive nearer death than life. We have no strength left.

We are silent with exhaustion. The euphoria we felt at dawn has finally gone. Has the last hope of rescue gone too? Who knows? We are so weak, we don't know any more.

Nobody talks. Our heads sink to our chests once more. Time passes slowly. With my eyes closed I get the dreams back, but this time broken up ... the gaps are bigger and bigger ... then nothing, just darkness.

Chapter 15

Windmills

Time goes by and we have no knowledge of its passing ...

I hear screams in the distance. Or is it yet another dream? Somebody shakes me violently and whispers ...

'Land! I can see land!'

It's Pavel, but I can hardly recognize his voice.

I try to follow his pointing finger. Precious time passes before I manage to heave my stiffened body into the right position. The dinghy is turning the wrong way. I cannot see anything but sea swell and racing dark clouds. Pavel stops shouting and only stares.

Hallucinations, I think. I try to calm him down.

'It's all right Pavliku. If there is land ... then surely we are safe ...'

Pavel stares into the distance for a while longer; perhaps he does not hear me. His head drops and he shuts his eyes. I look around for a bit longer and watch the passing clouds. Before the tiredness overcomes me I cannot help feeling alone with the dying and the dead. That's what I fear most.

How much longer can I hold on?

The sky suddenly falls back, black cloud passes by and it brightens up ... the curtain opens up ... and ...

Only a narrow strip of low ground is visible at first ... and on it a white windmill, its sails moving. I rub my eyes, but the image is still there.

'Pavle ... land!'

I shout and shout and shake him as best as I can.

With my other hand I keep pointing in the direction of the windmill.

By now we are at the bottom of a huge wave and the mountain of water prevents any view. When we reach the crest, all we see are racing clouds. Pavel stares at me, his look saying it all.

But we keep our heads up; we try desperately to stay alert. In silence we wait to reach the crest of the next huge wave. A few smaller ones pass us by and at last a huge wall of water approaches. When it reaches us, the force pushes our meagre craft to its top for a few seconds. That's enough.

'Land ... land!'

We both shout the word with the same feelings of the ship-wrecked from time immemorial.

It is true. In the distance a huge cloud draws back and we really see the magic strip of land with a white windmill. Its enormous sails keep turning; it's no hallucination.

We fix our eyes on this image, fearful of losing it again. We are excited. Our hearts pounding, we wait with bated breath.

The wave sweeps below us and we fall into its lap. The view disappears, the vision remains. We wonder where we've got to. We agree on Holland.

'But that's occupied by the Germans ...'

We try to check our pockets. We don't want them to find anything useful.

'So they'll get us. What does it matter?'

'If they decide to bump us off, it won't be too difficult.'

'It won't even hurt much Lojzku, I can't feel anything ...'

'Pavliku, still better to be buried in soil than feeding fish ... maybe they'll even put some flowers on our graves ...'

Our thoughts of the immediate future are disrupted by the sound of aircraft engines.

'Are they looking for us?'

The plane drops out of the clouds and heads for us.

'German, Junkers 88. I can see the swastika.'

The waiting is terrible. The plane carries on. The round out of the machine guns cuts through the engine noise. The water splashes quite close to us when the bullets hit the surface.

'You miserable sod! You call this brave ...' Pavel spits.

The plane turns and slowly departs. The engine noise dies down. Before we recover we hear another noise. Two Spitfires drop out of the clouds.

'Pavle ... they are ours!'

They chase after the Hun. Clouds lower over the land and the Spits soon disappear. We hear another round fired, perhaps they got him ...

The quick sequence of these events activates our last remaining energy. We wait for another ride on the crest. We must make sure that there is safety there.

These few moments are full of excitement and joy.

Our emotions are running high every time we see that strip of land getting nearer. The clouds are very low, almost touching the rough sea. The coast, as far as we can tell, is deserted.

The wind strengthens and the waves grow bigger.

The dinghy is virtually submerged. Scerba hangs on the ropes, his head on Mohr's chest, still unconscious.

'Pavle, we must get nearer that coast, otherwise we'll drown ...'

I stretch a piece of yellow canvas from the Mae West behind my back. Pavel opens up his flying jacket and together we create a sail of sorts to assist the wind.

It's hard. We are weak, our hands stiff but our will and hope of rescue pump new life into our bodies.

Even the brief moments of winter sunshine feel good.

The waves still grow. One carries us towards the coast; another returns us back to the sea. Sometimes we end up on the top of two adjoining crests. The dinghy hovers and falls to the bottom, once towards the coast, the other time back to the open sea. It's endless ...

From the crest of the waves our horizon broadens.

We can spot a few people running along the shore. Later we can make out individuals. More and more keep coming. Some wave their hands and point to the right. While on the top of another wave, we spot some wreckage. They are trying to warn us.

We attempt to turn our provisional sail as much as we can. It's exhausting; thirst demands another gulp of water. We resist it, we must survive now.

Not only the wind, but also our renewed hope pushes our dinghy nearer the shore.

At last we are close.

The crowd of people wait, men and women. We are almost there when another huge wave carries us out to the sea. It is unfair how the sea tries for the last time to claim us back. Eventually the waves bring us so close that a few men manage to grab the ropes. At that moment everything stops, even the sea pauses to acknowledge its defeat.

It's the land, which moves underneath us.

We are surrounded by deadly silence ...

Chapter 16

Terra Firma

Land – the magic word. How many times had we dreamt about it?

It did not receive us kindly, as if it did not want to accept what was almost taken by the sea. Pebbles and stones dug into our emaciated bodies through the thin wall of the dinghy.

As soon as we escaped the waves, out of the crowd came two German soldiers. They pushed through and aimed at us.

'Stand up!'

We neither moved nor replied.

Suddenly one of them threw his rifle on the ground, barked some orders and ran towards us. Some civilians followed. Together they pulled our dinghy from the reach of the sea.

They lifted us one by one out of the dinghy – farewell and thanks to our round wreck – and carried us to the nearby breakwater. The North Sea can be cruel.

All around us flat land with rows of windmills along the dykes.

Local fishermen's wives were holding white porcelain jugs full of fresh water to our lips – after so many days fresh water again. They cried, crossed themselves and stroked our heads.

They moved us into the big house close by, occupied by German soldiers, and laid us down on the floor, myself in the middle, Pavel and the unconscious Scerba on either side of me. We never saw Mohr's body again.

The room filled up. Noise, shouting, orders ... had they brought in the whole German Army?

At last they started to take off our clothes, trousers first. They had to cut them open only to reveal our hugely swollen legs, covered in blue and purple blotches, and deep, open, blackening wounds. The effect of the sea water!

'Yuck!' hissed the German corporal when he pulled off my trousers. At the same moment he spotted my RAF wings. He lost his rag.

'Englishman! Pilot!'

A soldier who until then was trying to revive Pavel's legs, jumped away and screamed, 'Bloody hell, I am sweating over him and he is a filthy Englishman!'

The doctor, who was trying to bring Scerba around, dressed the soldiers down. They kept quiet and continued for a bit longer. I turned to Pavel.

'We might loose our legs, but they probably won't shoot us. It's lucky there was no poison in that tin ...'

Scerba at last opened his eyes and wearily looked around, much to the doctor's relief. He ordered some warm drink to be brought; perhaps it was tea. It didn't matter as long as it was warm. Pavel and I had a drink but Scerba refused and nothing would change his mind. Later he told us why – he thought they wanted to poison him. They put us into an ambulance and the doctor sat with us.

'I overheard you talking Czech. My name is Doctor Braun. I studied in Prague and I am really pleased to meet my countrymen. I am not a Nazi, I am only following orders. I'll be happy to help you. We are going to Alkmaar, about 30 kilometres away.' He continued, 'I was in Prague at Christmas. A lot has changed. Prague is in turmoil; the Gestapo have arrested a lot of people. But Czechs are not so easily dissuaded, I know them well.'

We were glad when the journey came to an end. The doctor bid us farewell.

'If it weren't for Hitler ...'

We almost believed him. He got out as we reached our next destination.

Outside the Alkmaar naval hospital were two guards, their brisk steps piercing the evening calm. Snowflakes swirled around the front door light.

Soon after they carried us on stretchers into a room, the bell struck midnight. It was Sunday again, 4 January 1942.

Inside the hospital it was warm and comfortable. On top of that we were back amongst people, and at last sheltered. They put us into separate rooms.

A convent Sister kept washing my body, eyes welling up with tears. It felt as if my whole body was on fire, only the rest of my will, and fear of what was coming next, kept me conscious.

The thirst was back! I asked for some water but she only moistened my lips. Apparently I was not allowed to drink! Four doctors arrived. Checks, consultations, injections ...

I was hallucinating and in my mind I was again that straw between two big black lumps ...

The Sister gently lifted my legs and put new dressings underneath them.

'How awful!'

I heard that but had no idea who was talking. I could not believe that what I saw were actually my legs – shapeless, flesh falling off my ankles. My hands were also covered with ointment and dressings, slightly easing the burning pain.

The Sister left and a German soldier took her place. Why has he got a rifle? I wondered.

I asked for water. He came close and looked around briefly. Then he yelled, 'Englishman! Pilot!'

He grabbed my throat and tried to strangle me. The noise alerted the Sister and she got him off me.

Doctors returned and with them a priest but he could not get a lot out of me as I was losing consciousness. All my determination to hold on was useless. The black lumps rolled onto me and squashed that pathetic little straw ...

I heard some voices in my dream ... it also got lighter ... the sharp light irritated my eyes. I began to recognize my surroundings.

The Sister was leaning over me and moistened my lips. She was smiling through the tears. I wanted to ask where I was but could not utter a single word.

'Just lie still, don't talk. I will explain. Everything is fine now, nothing will happen to you. Your friends are also fine and waiting for you. You slept for a long time, three whole days. Your dead friend was buried ...'

So, that's it. Pepa is buried here ... in a foreign country ... and I could not say goodbye. I must come back here one day.

'You mustn't cry. Don't worry about anything now. Everything will be fine.'

She tried to comfort me but kept crying. Somebody wiped my forehead; I woke up again. Doctors were standing by my bed. They allowed me to have a shave but not to look at myself in the mirror.

*　*　*

100

A few days later they transferred us into the special German hospital for airmen in Amsterdam. They put the three of us into one room with a guard outside.

Doctors' visits were unusually frequent and often they spent a long time discussing something by my bed. At their recommendation I was put under some special dome-like cover – only my hands and head were outside – so my lower body had air circulation. The wounds on my legs became severely septic and stung. The worst time was when they changed my dressings and the cover had to be removed. Pavel and Josef's heads turned quickly. I felt sorry for them, and even the German nurse. He claimed that he'd rather volunteer for front-line duty. The stench became so overbearing that I lost my appetite and they had to put me on a drip. But the worse was to come – the areas around my open wounds blackened.

The doctors' diagnosis was gangrene which necessitated amputation of both legs!

I couldn't really take it all in as I was too weak by now.

'At least they won't hurt any more,' I managed to quip when the doctors left.

Pavel and Josef didn't say anything.

'You know, I could even dance again on some well-made artificial legs,' I tried to cheer myself up.

My friends did their best to keep my spirits up but struggled as they, too, needed some encouragement.

Eventually, in mid January, I was wheeled into the operating theatre. After an injection I was so out of it that I didn't really care. All I wanted was to sleep. Nurses were running around, doctors standing over my body. It felt as if I was watching all this from above . . . on the operating table was my body . . . my left leg marked above the knee and my right one just below . . .

The doctors still weren't happy. They kept prodding me and gave me yet another injection. My soul re-entered my body again and I dozed off.

When I came around, I was back in our room. They had not carried out the amputation – my poor general condition had prevented it.

For the next few days I went through a crisis, kept alive only by numerous injections. It wasn't life and it wasn't worth it – just basic overcoming of the suffering with no prospect for the future. The only bright moment of the day came at eight in the evening when I was given a large dose of morphine.

Some time later we had a visitor, an officer from German Intelligence. He took great care in noting all our details – serial number, nationality and our full names, which we had to give in accordance with the Geneva Convention. He finished writing and with a measurable degree of irony said, 'Scerba, Svoboda, Siska ... and you still claim that you are English? Don't be ridiculous. You really think that you are the first Czechs we've seen?'

Any Czech nationals who fought against Germany and were captured found themselves in a very tricky situation compared with other Allied soldiers. As citizens of the occupied territory they fell under Nazi jurisdiction. We rightly feared our fate.

'We admit we are not English born but as far as you are concerned you captured members of the Royal Air Force. You cannot deny it!'

'We'll see,' he grimaced. He probably had as much information about our own squadron as if he had served with the RAF.

I lifted the cover from my legs and the stench of the gangrene drove him out of the room.

During the evenings – when the air was 'clear' – we were visited by one of the doctors who came from Vienna. He fed us a load of propaganda from a German newspaper about the tonnage of Allied ships sunk and German success on the Russian Front. In return he wanted to hear from us details about the suffering imposed on the British people by Hitler's submarine blockade. When we told him the truth, he was deeply disappointed.

We were slowly regaining our strength and even my stomach settled down enough for me to start enjoying a bit of food. The gangrene that reached halfway up my calves, where it stopped, slowly began to heal. Black patches turned yellow and strange liquid oozed out. I started losing my hair fast.

Two weeks later the chief German doctor came to inspect me.

'Well, how are you doing after the amputation?'

Before I replied, the orderly lifted the cover and the doctor saw that my legs were still there.

'What's going on here? I sanctioned this amputation two weeks ago!'

Before his sidekick could open my file and explain from my notes what had actually happened, the chief doctor punished me with one day of fasting.

After he'd gone, the new doctor in charge of us stormed in.

'What a shambles! Why did you not report to me that you were due for amputation?'

'Nobody asked me ...'

'That's no excuse! As punishment, no morphine for you today.'

'I will get my own back on Hitler after the war for this,' I said to let off steam.

'What did this man say?' the doctor demanded as he made out Hitler's name.

'That your Führer's got the best doctors in the world,' Pavel quickly explained in German.

'But of course,' came the smooth reply and he added, turning to me, 'You should consider yourself lucky that you've still got your legs.'

Our nurse Lisa kept singing the same tune *'Denn wir fahren gegen England'* and started learning English.

'Why do you bother?' I asked.

'Hitler promised that we will be in England soon.'

'As prisoners of war, do you mean?'

She went bright red and lost her speech, but she can't have reported me as no punishment was meted out.

Time went by and soon it was Easter. On Easter Sunday I suddenly remembered the previous one I'd spent in prison, only then it was in the Citadel in Budapest. We wouldn't have known it was Easter Sunday had it not been for two ladies from the Dutch voluntary group who came to visit us, accompanied by the guards of course. They brought us some cakes and fruit. It was a complete surprise and we were quite moved. Fortunately we did not consume the food straight away, much to our advantage. What followed was like a scene out of *The Good Soldier Svejk* – as soon as the two ladies left, the guards stormed it and snatched everything they had given us. Judging by the way they went about it, they would have pumped out our stomachs as well, if we'd eaten any of it.

One day they brought in an English airman who was unconscious and bleeding from the mouth. When he had recovered consciousness, Pavel asked, 'Where did they get you?'

'We were attacking a German ship and hit the main mast. The plane exploded and sunk. I was fished out.'

'What were you flying?' I wanted to know.

'A Hudson from Coastal Command.'

That made us jump. We all wanted to find out whether he knew the squadron denoted by the letters RP.

'That's my squadron,' he replied without a pause.

'And the letter of your plane?' Scerba followed.

'I was a wireless operator on RP-P ...'

I could hardly control my voice.

'So that was you who found us in the North Sea! Why did you leave us?'

The Englishman – Bill Palmer – took a deep breath and started explaining.

'My one week leave started that Sunday, 28 December. When I came back a week later I found out that my crew and two others had taken part in a search operation just before New Year's Eve. RP-P reported sighting your dinghy about eighty-five miles east of Cromer. It reported your position to Yarmouth which sent out two speedboats. RP-P had to return, as it was low on fuel. The boats didn't find anything, although they kept searching for you all the next day, but without any luck. Then the weather worsened and the search was called off.'

So it was Bill Palmer's crew on RP-P who had found us, albeit they had had a different wireless operator with them as Bill was on leave. And the crew later died while attacking a German ship, with only Bill surviving.

Chapter 17

Prisoners of War

Time is the best healer, it is said. It goes by, heals the wounds, and reduces the suffering and the uncertainty. We were out of the worst and recovered enough to be moved.

One morning we found ourselves aboard the train to Germany. I was still too weak to sit up so was allowed to lie on the seat accompanied by a nurse.

When we arrived in Frankfurt-am-Main, during an air raid, the train stopped outside the station and the guards pushed everybody into the shelters. The nurse and I were the only two people left in our compartment.

'Why don't you go to the shelter?'

'My place is with the patient.'

I was surprised. Outside was complete mayhem. The anti-aircraft batteries were firing and bombs were exploding.

It was difficult to imagine how much was destroyed in those few minutes. When the all clear was sounded, the train could not proceed, so an ambulance took us to a small hospital in the town of Hohemarkt, which was part of the transit POW camp for airmen, Dulag Luft I. A German orderly took me to the second floor on his back, changed my clothes, put me to bed and locked the door. The unusual isolation was ominous, the overheated room became almost unbearable and my calls were not answered. The orderly came in the next morning and let some air in. After breakfast I had a visit from a German doctor.

'I have seen a lot of frostbite on the Russian front, but nothing like this. They should have cut those legs off. You will never walk on them again.'

I believed him as he spoke from experience. He was quite human, even sending the orderly for some ointment to cure my frost-bitten head. Then he covered me with a blanket again and locked me in.

The same day after lunch I had a visit from a Luftwaffe officer with an armband of the Red Cross on his sleeve. He brought with him some questionnaires and was very chatty. He knew far too much about the area where our airfield in England was situated.

'You must fill in these so you can receive parcels from the Red Cross,' he said and put a pile of papers down with a pen and few English cigarettes.

The questionnaire contained a lot of questions of a purely military nature, so I filled in my name, my number and my nationality – British of course – trying to follow the Geneva Convention as before.

The officer returned the next day, glanced at the blank question-naire and changed his tune. He swore at me, threatened me, and eventually took the papers and the cigarettes, and left.

Two days later a civilian brought in the same questionnaire and kindly offered to fill them in for me; I only had to answer the ques-tions. I thanked him for his kindness and pointed out that I had already fulfilled my duty. I could not resist asking whether he would agree to a German officer being asked such questions if he were imprisoned in England. He did not answer.

Neither of these two had mentioned my nationality, although the civilian warned me about my position in a victorious Germany.

But he did not succeed and left – while I naively believed that was the end of it.

A few days later the peace and quiet was suddenly disturbed by shouting outside my room.

'Where is that Czech dog?'

There was a commotion outside the door, somebody unlocked it and a furious officer with green lapels came in. He bent over me waving some papers in his hand and screamed, 'How dare you not fill in these questionnaires? Remember you are in Germany. We have ways to make you to co-operate!'

That was a bit much. I pulled off the cover and the room filled with the horrible stench.

'Be my guest!'

I waited. The German officer jumped away from my bed, spat, threw the papers on the floor and, swearing, left the room. The orderly picked up the papers and left too.

This was the first time they reminded me of my real nationality.

On the ninth day they moved me to a lower floor and put me in with Pavel and Josef, both of whom had also been interrogated.

There were several other rooms on this floor, full of wounded airmen. As soon as they recovered they were sent to POW camps and their places taken by new arrivals.

We reported the circumstances of our interrogation to the senior British officer in the hospital and he promised to report the case to Geneva HQ via the Protecting Powers body.

We saw many British wounded airmen in this small hospital who brought us news of more modern planes and a rising number of raids over Germany. This was a real morale booster. Meanwhile, the obligatory German newsreels, their special news bulletins, were becoming sparser now. The usual millions of tons of sunken Allied shipping turned into 'mere' thousands. Only Goebbels kept shouting and swearing at the Anglo-American air pirates. Most important was the news that German forces were retreating on the Russian Front back to 'safe' positions.

These were happy facts, which allowed us to forget temporarily our situation and look forward to a better future.

My legs? So far the assessment made by the German doctor had proved correct – they should have cut them off.

'You will never walk on them again,' he'd said. I was beginning to agree with him. But legs are not everything; one could live without them after all.

I had been confined to my bed for almost six months when, one day, I managed to sit up without anybody's help. True, I collapsed back into bed after a few minutes from sheer exhaustion, but I fought back quickly.

Using crutches proved more difficult and they had to bandage my legs together so I was, in fact, moving on three legs. But the feeling of life returning – that was difficult to describe! When I managed to crawl to the toilet on my own one day, I was as happy as Larry.

Pavel Svoboda and Josef Scerba had both recovered well enough by the end of June to be transported to different POW camps for

British soldiers. We parted company crying – it was the last time I saw either of them during my years of captivity.

At the end of the summer of 1942 I was transferred to the hospital at Obermansfeld, together with two other English prisoners. The old building, originally an agricultural college, was full of members of the British Expeditionary Force from Dunkirk; amongst them were scores of men without arms or legs, some with both limbs missing on the same side of the body.

There were also two Finnish sailors whose ship had been sunk by a German sub. They survived on a small boat but both lost their legs to frostbite.

I had never before seen so much suffering, though none of these men were down in spirit or morose. Each bit of good news from the front line made them incredibly happy. There was lots of talk about the post-war world order. The priest, an English padre, read words of comfort and hope from the Bible every week during Sunday service. The British national anthem at the end of it was a welcome reminder of Sundays spent in England. A large group of Australian soldiers criticized British politics, including the fate of Czechoslovakia and the Munich Agreement.

The Germans did not like such discussion as it got on their nerves and did their best to disrupt them by carrying out searches. They saw illegal activity behind everything.

I was the only Czech at Obermansfeld and perhaps for that reason I was always under suspicion as being the instigator of any illegal action. I had a lot of attention from one ginger-haired corporal. Often he and his men would carry me into his office and strip-search me. When they took me back to my room again, my bed would be in a mess and the mattress cut up. I then had to mend it but at least it gave me something to do. Needless to say, they never found anything.

We always carefully hid any news that came in via the work parties, which met with forced labour from Czechoslovakia, France and Poland – usually inside any bandage, gathering any snippets of information for those who were planning to escape. After successful escapes – which were usually not discovered for several days – the Germans went mad, turned everything upside down, and the daily regime became stricter for a while.

It was here I had an operation on the veins in my left calf. The gangrene was still troubling me.

Weeks went by and more prisoners arrived, now mainly airmen. One day they brought in a wounded Scottish priest who'd been a crew member of a plane that was shot down. He only had a broken arm, which was already in plaster. A few days later he was expecting a transfer into an ordinary POW camp. He was a well-built man who had met a lot of Czechs while doing his parachute training with his unit, and liked them. When he found out that I was Czech too, he pressed me to escape with him. He reassured me that he would carry me on his back for as long as it would take it. I happily believed him and agreed to go with him.

We had to wait, however, as I was still recovering from my operation. The German board which decided who was fit to be transferred to POW camps was due to meet just a few days before my stitches were due to be taken out. The English doctors promised to do their best to keep the Scot amongst the sick until the next meeting two weeks later.

In the meantime we were getting ready for our escape. Our aim was to get back to my homeland and join a unit of the underground. We planned to travel on coal trains, hiding under the coal, for which we made simple breathing masks with a piece of tube. We hoarded what food we could and the British doctors supplied us with all the medication that we needed.

The day of the meeting came. The German doctor in charge dismissed the findings of the British doctors and declared the Scot fit, which meant only one thing – transfer to the POW camp Oflag IX C the next day. Our planned escape was crushed.

The priest decided that he would try and escape en route, I wished him well and we said our goodbyes.

The group being moved wasn't big: three prisoners and three guards, who were led by the ginger-haired Corporal, otherwise known as the Ginger Dog. We all hoped the Scot would succeed in his attempt as it would make the Corporal's life difficult and he might even not come back.

The next day the train guards brought the Scot back – in chains. The doctors changed his plaster and he was moved to a POW camp the same afternoon. I later learned from the doctor that the Scot jumped out of the moving train, but unfortunately for him he landed amongst some workers repairing the track, and they caught him.

The Ginger Dog returned three days later and made his presence known.

The next meeting of the German medical board was even bigger and their aim was to choose the most serious cases for proposed repatriation.

I was amongst those chosen and we were transported to another transit camp in a big monastery at Kloster Haina near Kassel. We slept in a huge hall with columns, sixty-two beds and forty blind men. It was unbelievable how much energy they had, and the will to live, after three years of darkness.

Jim came from Scotland. He trained as a masseur and passed his exam in front of the international jury with flying colours. It was a delight to watch him in the morning. He got up singing or whistling, picked up his shaving kit and towel, and off he went. He walked in between the beds, avoided the columns and got into the washroom where he washed and shaved as if he could see.

What can he see? I often wondered. Perhaps the dunes at Dunkirk, long queues of soldiers scattered on the open beach, their struggle to the boats in water up to their chins ... the appearance of a German plane, a few explosions and the last glimpse of light ... Jim, what if all the powerful men in the world had to stand in full kit on the beach with no other way out and desperately waiting for rescue?

One day I met him in the narrow corridor in between the beds and offered to help. He thanked me but refused in a way which put me off offering help to any of them in the future. They were all very independent and lived their lives in their own world.

Another prisoner, Major Charles, had been an eye specialist before the war and successfully operated on a blind boxer called Ted, who had been blind for three years. Before the operation he often entertained us in his typical way. He would play the 'Last Post' on his clarinet in the evening, impersonating the angel, standing naked on one leg. After he regained his sight, he grew quiet and melancholic. I asked what had changed.

'I think I was happier while I was blind. I had more freedom of mind. The surroundings did not affect me. You know, Louis, I got used to not seeing all this misery and suffering ...'

I tried to comfort him. 'What's around us now, Ted, and it's all wrong, but it's only temporary. When the war is over, all this will be over too. And we will be fine again.'

He stared into the distance and replied, 'Let's hope so, Louis, let's hope.'

Ted lived in hope and so did I . . .

The prisoners formed a band and they knew how to play! Their piano player used the organ – only when the Germans allowed it, of course – and the music touched all of us, even the Germans . . . until they heard the first notes of 'Roll Out The Barrel' – then they woke up and with the usual 'Los! Los!' forced us out of the chapel.

That would not do – English prisoners in Germany playing such a tune when the Russian Front was falling apart . . .

Chapter 18

Sagan

We waited for the next meeting of the international repatriation committee with anticipation. The German chief doctor visited us every week and made recommendations which were dutifully noted by his sidekick, Captain Jung. There it stopped.

The committee sat on 23 October 1942. It was chaired by one Swiss and one Swedish doctor, with American and British doctors as representatives of the Allied forces at the Red Cross on one side, and on the other the German military doctors.

My number, thirty-three, was called. They sat me in front of a big table on a stool. As the Germans got their case notes ready, the Swedish doctor walked over to me.

'What have you got there?' he asked in English and with disbelief pointed at my legs. I explained that I had suffered severe frostbite and how it had happened.

The Scandinavian turned to the Germans.

'You call yourselves humans? Take a look at this patient. What have you done for him? Why didn't you send him to a neutral country where he would have received appropriate treatment?'

The Germans put their heads together and conferred briefly. Their senior doctor replied, 'We have got the best experience with frostbite from the Russian Front. We can take care of him. I propose to postpone this case until the next meeting.'

The others, after some deliberation, agreed. I was given a piece of paper for the next meeting, which was – in six months' time.

Those who were considered suitable for repatriation were moved and their places taken by new arrivals.

* * *

The following Sunday Doctor Jung quite unexpectedly had me brought in to his office and sat me on a stool. This was unusual as medical examinations of all patients normally took place by their beds. Two British doctors, who were also prisoners, were already there.

Jung turned over the pages of my notes and after a moment or two asked where I actually came from. The first interpreter said that I was Polish.

'No, he is Czech,' said the second one.

I wondered where all this was leading.

'So why isn't he in the Luftwaffe as some of his countrymen?' the doctor asked. The interpreters didn't dare answer this question, so they translated it for me.

'Would you tell your doctor that such questions are against the Geneva Convention? However, I think I made the right decision to fight on the other side.'

You could hear a pin drop.

The doctor suddenly jumped from his chair, reached for me and started pulling off the bandages, with the skin attached. He shouted, 'Walk! Walk!'

I asked the interpreter to point out that even he should realize that I couldn't walk on those legs. As Jung got even more angry I turned to one of the British doctors and asked him to explain my medical condition. Captain Dickie tried in his good German to explain, but Jung snapped at him, 'I didn't ask you! You are prisoners here and I am the boss!'

That was more than the normally composed British officer could take. He grabbed the shoulder of one of the interpreters and demanded, 'Tell your doctor that I am responsible to the British Government for this patient.'

He was about to say something else when Jung opened the door and ordered him out. He then turned to the two guards and ordered them to stand me up. To my surprise, neither of them moved.

Jung yelled, 'Did you hear me!'

Only then did those two front-line veterans click their heels and, holding me under my arms, stand me up. Jung went mad.

'Pull him backwards and forwards! I will teach you to walk, you Czech bastard!'

They pulled me away from the stool, leaving behind a trail of blood and puss.

'Let him go!'

I collapsed and the second British doctor, Major Charles, tried to intervene, but the German ignored him completely.

'Stand up! Walk! Stand up! Walk!' shouted Jung, pushing away the guards who were standing over me looking rather lost.

Only thanks to the courage and experience of the British orderlies who picked me up and virtually kidnapped me was I saved. It felt like eternity before I was back in my bed.

The British doctors managed to report this blatant breach of the rules directly to Geneva and a few days later two representatives arrived, one Swede and one Swiss. They listened carefully to the whole story and declared, 'If we intervene on your behalf, it could actually jeopardize your safety further. You're in Germany and they could kill you quite easily. But we will exercise all our diplomatic powers to ensure that all prisoners are treated strictly according to the uniform they are wearing when captured, and not according to their original nationality.'

After they had left Jung ordered that I should be checked several times a night using a powerful light. Before the Germans grew tired of this latest trick, I'd got used to it ...

Christmas came, then spring and by the time summer was upon us the whole incident was forgotten; even the fear had gone. In mid-1943 I was told to get ready for a journey. Nobody seemed to know where to or who would accompany me. Eventually I was taken into the office and handed over to three members of the Wehrmacht, which pleased me as soldiers were always easier to get on with.

Much to my pleasure they also decided to send along another prisoner, a junior officer from Canada, and we all went to the station by horse and cart.

The journey did not start particularly well as the behaviour of the Germans towards us and their rather abrupt manners were worrying. But after a few hours their attitude changed, mainly thanks to a supply of English cigarettes. The senior one amongst them resisted for a while, but in the end he gave in and the other two happily followed. That way we made sure none of them would talk, as it was strictly forbidden for German guards to accept cigarettes from prisoners.

Before they had finished their first cigarette, we found out that we were going to Stalag Luft III at Sagan.

We had to change trains at Halle and our next one was not due to leave until the following morning, so the two junior guards looked after us while their boss went to find some accommodation. When he came back he guided us to a labour camp for Ukrainians on the edge of the town. It was late afternoon and the streets were deserted; the atmosphere was very oppressive.

I dragged myself along on my crutches using my legs as props. I suffered badly and had to rest every few steps. Eventually the guards created a makeshift stretcher out of the crutches and carried me. In the camp we were allocated a floor space in the corner of a hut. My legs felt terrible!

The journey from the station took a lot out of me and I could hardly stand up on the crutches. The senior guard, with the help of more English cigarettes, arranged that two Ukrainians would take me back to the station on a two-wheel cart. The next day was a beautiful Sunday morning and there was a crowd of people outside the station, mainly women. Where were they all going? Not many uniforms were in view.

I gave each Ukrainian a packet of cigarettes for their help. A friend of mine had given them to me before I left hospital, and I'd kept them just in case.

But I made a mistake – I didn't realize that cigarettes at that time were a precious commodity in Germany. Somebody in the crowd saw my gesture and protested that it was unfair that Russian prisoners were given cigarettes when German soldiers in the front line did not have any. Others joined in with 'Take them back.' I pointed out that they were my cigarettes and that they were a gift from me. Why didn't I keep quiet? Somebody shouted, 'Englishman! Pilot!'

The crowd made a sudden move towards us. God knows what would have happened if the senior guard had not known his own people. He pulled out his pistol and shouted, 'Stop! Get back!'

The other two followed suit and two guards from the labour camp shielded the Ukrainians.

But they took away the cigarettes, the crowd stopped shouting and we got inside the station under the cover of our guards.

The train was late and the crowd soon calmed down. When it eventually arrived, the people poured on and emptied the platform in seconds. The senior guard kept looking for a compartment allocated for prisoners but there wasn't one, so he went to the conductor who was about to signal for the train to leave and remonstrated with him. The conductor ignored him and gave the signal for the engine driver to leave.

'We aren't going anywhere,' I commented.

Wrong. The senior guard did not take no for an answer and ran the length of the train with his pistol in his hand shouting, 'Stop!' When he reached the steps of the engine he pointed the gun at the driver. 'This train is not leaving until I get a special compartment.'

The driver protested, the conductor blew his whistle but our guard insisted, 'We do the fighting, we issue the orders!'

The train didn't move, but in the end a woman conductor vacated part of her compartment in the service carriage, and we set off.

The compartment was divided into two. The conductor and her two colleagues were on one side and we were on the other. We praised our senior guard for his effort and lit a cigarette.

We smoked in silence as there wasn't anything to talk about. Not so the women. They wouldn't stop, especially one of them. 'She went on,' my Canadian companion quipped, 'like a bloody machine gun.'

The senior guard acknowledged this sentiment with a smile and said in English, 'Yes, yes.' Suddenly we had something in common.

The women went quiet. Did they understand English? Oh yes, they did. One of them got up and ordered the senior guard to stand to attention.

'You mocked me in front of the prisoners. I finish my shift at the next station. You will come with me to the station office and sign a statement.'

The train stopped at Leipzig. The conductor stepped out and our guard had to go with her. He came back half an hour later, white as a chalk, hands shaking and looking scared.

We were some way away from the station before he told us, 'She really made it hard for me. I might even be sent to the Russian Front.' The fear in his voice said it all. Well, I thought, you are beginning to reap what you have sown.

The rest of the journey was uneventful.

At Sagan, the biggest POW camp for airmen inside the Third Reich, they handed us over to the German Commanding Officer.

A thorough search and detailed examination of our documents followed, and then they split us up. They took the Canadian away and locked me up in a small room near the German headquarters. It was sparsely furnished with just a wooden bed, water jug and a bucket and it happened so suddenly and unexpectedly that I did not even protest. I was terribly tired, couldn't think straight and just wanted to lie down. It was only during that night that I realized Doctor Jung had got his own back ...

The next morning a German guard brought me a mug of a brown liquid and a piece of dark bread. He had no idea why I was locked up.

My wounds were still open so I asked for a doctor. He didn't come until a day later so I demanded to be seen by the senior British officer – unsuccessfully.

Chapter 19

Arrest

After ten days I was moved to Stalag Luft I, the POW camp for airmen in Barth on the Baltic coast. Surprisingly, after the customary check, I was allowed to join the other airmen, amongst them fifteen Czechoslovaks. We shared a hut and had a lot to talk about.

The camp's second in command was Captain von Muller, an intelligence officer, who reportedly had a smallholding somewhere in Bohemia. He wasn't too bad. As there had been a lot of escapes from the camp, the prisoners were not forced to work. They counted us at least twice a day, each roll call lasting a good two hours. I reported to the British Commanding Officer in the camp.

It was a welcome and pleasant change to be amongst my own countrymen and amongst healthy men again. I received a sincere welcome – our crash and several days' ordeal in the dinghy commanded a lot of respect.

After three days a German orderly, otherwise known as a 'ferret', approached me and said, 'Captain von Muller wishes to speak to you.'

My previous experience called for caution, but I was curious to find out what it was about. This von Muller – would he be different? He certainly took rather a long time to read my personal file before calling me in.

Down the corridor of the German camp headquarters the interpreter knocked on the door and went in first, closely followed by me. He announced my name and stepped back.

Behind the desk sat an air force officer in a very smart uniform. He stood up, smiled and offered his hand with a well pronounced 'Welcome'.

I had prepared myself for all sorts of things, but I had not expected this. I therefore stood silently, leaning forward on my crutches. The Nazi withdrew his hand and with it the smile, and sat down before continuing briskly, 'We badly need your home address. We need to fill in your personal records in case we need to contact your parents or relations.'

Nice try. Never mind, I'd seen worse.

'I've fulfilled my duty by giving my name, number and nationality. I have nothing to add.'

'But we know you are Czech as well as your friends in the camp. You can't deny it.'

'I'm denying nothing, but as far as you are concerned I am a British prisoner.'

The more he tried to persuade me about the advantages of answering all his questions, the more I remembered my previous encounters. I began to get angry.

'I wasn't born yesterday, you know.'

I said nothing more after that. He watched me for a moment and waited – nothing?

Then he let me go saying, 'You'll regret this.'

More prisoners kept arriving, amongst them a lot of Americans, and with them came the latest news about the situation at the front, which was distinctly in favour of the Allies. They took their imprisonment lightly, convinced that it would all be over soon. When the weather and the Germans permitted, they played baseball and rugby. Some of them took up studying while others came up with the sort of crazy ideas that can only happen in a confined environment. They even tried to invent things although they had nowhere to test them. I took up watch repairing, first from books I had received through the Red Cross, and later experimenting on other people's watches. I found I was surprisingly good at it and was even invited to America after the war, with the promise of quick financial reward.

A lot of time was devoted to thinking up escape plans. Although the Germans could detect the classic ones like tunnels fairly easily – they had both the knowledge and sound detectors – the prisoners thought up all sorts of options, such as hiding in the sewage cart which was brought to the camp by Polish prisoners. The Nazi

'*Ubermenschen*' of course distanced themselves from this job. The trick was not to lower the hose into the septic tank too far so that it only sucked up air, thereby leaving enough room for a few prisoners to get inside the cart. It was not a pleasant ride, but the desire to escape outweighed the unpleasantness.

When the Germans found out, we came up with something else. How about dressing up as the guard unit and walking out just before the change of shifts? The stumbling block was the need for thirteen complete uniforms including the same number of guns and one pistol. Here the renowned Czech skill came to its own. Some of us made uniforms out of army issue blankets, luckily the same colour as the uniforms. Others made wooden replica guns. Another group of prisoners took on watching and recording the times and pattern of the guard movements around the camp. The biggest difficulty was matching the uniform buttons, buckles, uniform and cap badges.

It was nearly Christmas 1943 and the escape committee halted all other attempts. Nobody minded much; after all it was too cold.

The escape plan was almost ready. The German Camp Commandant was pleased that nobody had escaped for two months and rewarded us with three musicians to entertain us on New Year's Eve. They duly came and played – on their departure they were short of a cap, a belt and some buttons.

Some New Year's Eve!

Soon after their departure the Germans rushed in with search dogs. The dogs sniffed and sniffed, soldiers turned over all the beds and threatened us, but they found nothing. They repeated this routine several times, but eventually gave up. In the meantime we kept collecting every piece of tin foil from cigarette packets to manufacture the missing items. We made the moulds out of plaster using the samples we had stolen from the musicians.

At last the spring of 1944 arrived and it got warmer.

An Englishman called Charlie, a pre-war teacher and navigator from a bomber, was appointed the Commanding Officer of the guard unit. He fitted the role, both in stature and his looks. There was as much excitement as before a first night performance, but there was no opporunity for a final rehearsal. And so one afternoon as soon as the special watch reported the guard unit passing the last watchtower, our replacement unit marched into the space in proper military formation. Everything we dressed those lucky thirteen in was so good – as was their performance – that they passed through the gate.

When the last gate opened in front of them, they met some higher-ranking officer. They saluted as expected, but he stopped them and asked where they were going. They had not prepared for such an eventuality and Charlie had no answer for him.

Yes, it all failed at the last gate and the thirteen got thirty days of solitary confinement.

The rest of us were summoned for a roll call and personally checked against our records with the help of extra guards. It was getting dark when they checked the last prisoner and were left with thirteen unaccounted cards – the escapees were already in the cells.

'That's in order,' announced von Muller and when he ordered the gates to the huts to be opened, 2,000 hungry and thirsty men made for them with a massive roar. As the guards made their way back to the watchtowers, three prisoners took advantage of the general mayhem and escaped.

The next morning the Germans could not get the numbers to tally, so we had another full roll call. It was not particularly pleasant for us, but the Germans did not enjoy it either. They did their best to prevent as many escapes as possible.

They even printed special posters saying: 'Those caught escaping, will be shot immediately.' This contravened the Geneva Convention and one American Air Force officer promptly pulled down one of the posters in front of a German guard. The guard blew his whistle and the American was brought in front of the German Camp Commandant. He apparently faced a German military court.

Another year of captivity went by ...

By the summer of 1944 the Germans were beginning to panic. We all felt the end of the war nearing inexorably. We lived in hope, all the suffering and deprivation paling in comparison to this.

And my legs? They were still septic – mainly the left one. This resulted in another move, this time to a prisoner-of-war hospital at Neubrandenburg. There were several hundred Belgian soldiers and even a Russian prisoner (the only survivor from a death march of several thousand), who had lost his legs. He told us about his mates who had contracted typhoid. The Germans shot the dying ones and buried them in two huge holes in the ground – some still alive.

I underwent an operation, which was carried out by Polish naval doctors. The next day was beautiful and sunny with a cloudless sky. At ten o'clock the siren sounded in the town below.

A few minutes later we saw the first wave of the four-engined bombers with a strong fighter escort. From above came different fighters and soon we heard the first rattle of firing. The German attack failed, however, and the Allied fighters forced them into battle. We saw the first burning planes falling as white mushrooms of parachutes popped up against the sunlit sky and white lines of smoke lingered behind the stricken planes. When it was all over, the sky was covered with a continuous white cloud.

The first prisoners arrived that afternoon. They put an American next to me with a shrapnel wound to his face. It didn't seem serious and he was able to talk.

'The Focke Wulfs attacked us from the sun. We fired our 50 mm guns when the plane shook ... third engine caught fire ... I could not see ... cabin was full of black smoke ... I was choking ... we left our formation as bits of burning plane flew past us ...'

He did not finish the sentence as he was starting to bleed from his mouth. The doctors could do nothing. Shrapnel had cut his artery and he bled to death.

Another one came in with a broken arm. He told us how his crew members had been beaten to death by civilians, who'd reached them before the soldiers. Altogether they brought in seventeen American airmen from various planes that afternoon. There should have been about a hundred of them, but most of them did not make it ...

A few days later a horse and cart came to pick me up. The Polish doctors objected to the mode of transport as unsuitable but the German Commandant was not prepared to listen – the order obviously came from above.

They laid me on a thin layer of straw and took me to the station. I was grateful to them for covering me with blankets as my uniform had the same effect on the local population as a red rag to a bull.

I travelled under guard in a separate compartment to the POW camp at Barth where they put me into the surgical ward. Once they had taken the stitches out they put me in with the other prisoners.

Rumours were circulating round the camp that Hitler had been assassinated. We waited anxiously to see whether Himmler would take over Germany and replace the existing Wehrmacht guards with his own.

The second day after my arrival in the camp I was escorted by the usual 'ferret' to the Commandant's office. A major in the German Secret Police (*Sicherheistdienst*) pulled out some document and asked me to sign it.

'I cannot sign anything without the British Commanding Officer present,' I protested.

'It's only a formality.'

'Take it back to the camp. I will only sign it in the Commanding Officer's presence,' I insisted.

'This document cannot leave my office,' he snapped.

It was pretty obvious that this was no formality so I did not sign it. The Major started shouting and threatening me. Referring to my 'Third Reich' nationality, he told me, 'Because of that, it is your duty to sign this document and obey the German authorities. Otherwise you will face the consequences.'

The situation was heating up fast.

'For you I remain a British prisoner.'

'Attention!' the officer ordered and the two typists jumped up. He read the document in a loud voice and asked the interpreter to translate it into English for me. After that he ordered the typists to countersign it to confirm its authenticity.

It was an order for my arrest ...

They took me straight to the solitary cell and from that moment I was under arrest. After several uncomfortable hours on a wooden bunk and hard thinking about my new situation, I fell asleep. It got colder after midnight. I could hear the sound of an air raid in the distance. For somebody it meant the beginning of the end, but I drifted off with new hope ...

Chapter 20

The Gestapo Move In

After a month in prison I was moved to Berlin. While changing trains in Strasslund, my British uniform provoked such a violent response from the crowd that my escort and even the railway station guards had to protect me.

On the next leg of my journey I found myself in the company of another six Czechoslovak airmen and a heavy escort, all travelling on a night train to an unknown destination.

During that journey an incident occurred. The commander of our small group – this time an officer – could not find our reserved compartment in the overcrowded and dimly lit train, but he did find one occupied by officers returning from the front. When he woke them up and asked them to vacate the compartment, one of them, an officer senior to ours, raised his voice, whereupon our officer showed him some document, which he read by torchlight. The impact was amazing – the front-line soldier changed his tune and asked his companions to vacate the compartment. What was in that document, we wondered? But our escorts were very cagey.

At five in the morning the train stopped at the station of Usti nad Orlici – we were back in our own country, which took us by surprise. When we asked for some water the guards allowed us out of the train in pairs, and with the obligatory escort we went to the station well for a drink. Some woman was just filling a big jug and one of our escorts suggested that we ask to borrow it, which we did, in Czech. She looked afraid and ran away. The guard sneered, 'There you are. That's your own people for you. They would not even give you a drink of water.'

I got angry – not with the woman, but with those who had humiliated our nation and filled their hearts with fear.

We reached Prague the same afternoon. It was Tuesday, 22 August 1944.

Our guards waited until the platform was empty but there were still a lot of people outside the station and some of them noticed us. They stopped and kept looking at us. We overheard them saying, 'English pilots ...'

How we wanted to shout, 'We are Czechs, real Czechs!' Some of us were even from Prague ... but now we knew what would follow. So we staggered silently down the park away from the station. We had no idea where they were taking us – it did not matter. Suddenly we stopped.

'Stop! Wait here!'

To our surprise the officer went into the Hotel Esplanade but was soon back. Presumably the two SS men standing guard at the front door confused him. We moved on a bit further and stopped in front of a big corner building, which was originally known as the Petschka Palace, but now was the Gestapo headquarters in Prague. I'd heard stories about it in the camps.

A short time before we still held out some hope that things would not be so bad, but this was a definite turn for the worse, as we knew full well that if we remained in the hands of the Wehrmacht, our situation would not be entirely hopeless. The sudden uncertainty was overwhelming – we could not even think straight. The guards handed us over inside the building and left.

Our new Gestapo guards forced us into a lift, took us up to the fourth floor and shoved us into a tiny room.

It was hot. A young pale-faced blond woman in a thin low-cut dress sat at the desk with a cigarette in her mouth, gazing at us. She made a few comments in Czech until a Gestapo man came in from another room. He did not like something about her and unceremoniously ordered her out.

'Face the wall, all of you!' he shouted suddenly, and slapped Eman Novotny so hard that he knocked me down. I, in turn, knocked down the others. We stood up again and the Gestapo man smacked our heads against the wall.

Hungry and thirsty, we stood in the heat of the room until that evening, with no interrogation, no explanation. When their henchmen came for us, we were at the end of our tether.

They ordered us into a Black Maria, locked us in and drove us through the streets of Prague. We were exhausted and hoped that our next stop might be a bit more pleasant than the Petschka Palace.

At last we stopped. After a lot of shouting in German and barking of orders, someone unlocked the van.

'*Los! Los!*'

More shouting and hands emerging from black uniforms, throwing us out onto the ground.

I was last out – what would happen to me? Before I could do anything I bumped into one of the guards. More kicking.

We were in no doubt that we were in the yard of the German interrogation prison at Pankrac. With more shouting they pushed us towards the entrance hall. In the middle of a wide staircase stood a man in a black shirt and polished boots, well fitting his physique. I gazed in wonder as I tried to remember in which pantomime I had seen such a character, until the Czech policeman pushed me towards the counter where I was told to leave my clothes. He shouted just like the Germans. Another one behind the counter demanded I undress and threw me some stripey trousers and a tunic.

'These rags in exchange for my uniform? Never!'

I resisted the demanding hands of the policeman with all my strength, which was obviously too much even for the figurine on the stairs. He grabbed me and swiftly unbuttoned my uniform, perhaps wanting to punish me for my audacity at looking him over when we came in, instead of obediently staring at his boots.

Curiosity, or perhaps the noise, brought in some higher ranking officer. Arguments followed, but we kept our uniforms. Was it a victory? They did not normally give up for nothing.

They took us to the cells. I was number seventy-five. They did not bother much about living space – the four of us had to make do with a cell for one.

We had had previous experiences with different cells on our journey to England, but that was not much help at Pankrac. The Nazis were real masters of this craft.

The regime was tough. On top of this I had to endure a stream of abuse and threats because I had dared to lie down during the day. I could not help it – my legs were not up to it yet.

At six in the morning on the third day I had to shave with the door open and then stand with my face to the wall. After a while they called my number and told me to stand with my face to the wall by the staircase. I progressed in this manner all the way up to the ground floor where I joined another eleven men.

One three-digit number was called a second time but nobody answered. A Czech policeman approached an older man standing in the front row and told him to go in. He must have known him already. The man was shaking badly and could not even repeat his number. A Gestapo man pushed me aside and with a bunch of keys hit the man over his head several times. The prisoner fell to the ground, blood pouring out of his head.

I felt dizzy again, so I turned round and sat on the bench nearby. That was too much for the Gestapo man. I'd never before seen anybody actually foaming with anger. He simply wasn't used to a prisoner behaving in such a way and kept screaming into my face, but he had to give up as I was not used to his behaviour. When he ordered me to stand facing the wall, I replied in English that I was unwell and remained seated.

Eventually the gates opened again and the Black Maria took us away. We had no idea where we were being taken to but recognized the inner courtyard of the Petschka Palace. They took us into a large room which resembled an auditorium and which was also used as a prayer room or a cinema.

They sat me down in the third row behind two rows of young girls. The rest of us had to sit half a metre apart. A Czech policeman patrolled in between the rows and made sure nobody moved. In front of us, on a raised platform, sat a Gestapo man behind a desk. He was nodding off. My neighbour on the right whispered, 'Zigaretten?'

He obviously did not realize that I was Czech. I pretended that I was adjusting my bandage and pushed a few cigarettes his way.

He must have been a heavy smoker or perhaps he had not had a cigarette for a long time because he grabbed them too quickly. The Czech policeman noticed and took the cigarettes off him. He then moved him towards the back of the room and stood him against the wall. The man was lucky – if a German had noticed, it would have been much worse for both of us.

I was ordered to sit on my own on a small bench on the right. Somebody had left a farewell message on the wall, probably using a nail ...

Given my circumstances I did not find such a message from the brink of death very inspirational, but I wasn't too disturbed by it. All

127

of us who chose to fight had to accept that death was part of it, but I felt sorry for those who were left with this last chance to express their feelings, or worse for those who did not even get this last chance.

A Gestapo man came in, exchanged me for a piece of paper and took me up in the lift. I decided that I would feign memory loss from now on.

Six interrogators went for me quite abruptly. I tried to give the impression that any questions regarding my family and myself did not apply to me. I stared glumly at them and kept silent, but it did not help much as some of them were losing their patience and became rather rude. One of the more mild-mannered interrogators showed me some documents and my personal record including my photograph from my last place of work.

'Do you recognize this? It's you, isn't it?'

He proceeded to name all the members of my family and stressed that my mother was in one of their hospitals at present, suffering from pneumonia. He tried hard to refresh my memory and knew how to go about it.

It was nerve-racking. On the one hand, according to the rules, I was only expected to give them my name and number, which I had already done. And now I refused to recognize my own photograph. On the other hand, they had my mother ...

My head started spinning as the questions flowed fast. I protested.

'If you know all this, why do you keep on asking?'

'You ran away and you were spotted at Bratislava railway station on the 5th January 1940. We want to know how you managed to get there? You must have had a travel permit for the Slovak State. Who gave it to you?'

From these questions I concluded that they did not actually know any details about my escape. I did not of course have a permit. I calmed down a bit and decided to lead them along a different escape route from the one I'd actually taken.

'I went by train via the towns of Zlin, Vizovice and continued to Slovakia ...'

They did not think it possible and did not believe me. I insisted and claimed that I could not remember anything else.

One of them left the room and brought back a map of the old Czechoslovakia. They studied over it for a while and in those few precious moments without questions, I managed to regain a bit of my strength and confidence.

I gained even more respite as one of them stated that I could quite easily have travelled by local train via Vizovice. Little did he know that the railway line to Lutonina, already marked on the map, was in fact never completed – it was part of the work opportunity for the unemployed during the 1930s. I knew – I had worked there myself. This little victory cheered me up.

They took me to another room in which a middle-aged woman sat by a desk. I greeted her and thought that she smiled faintly. It felt like a refuge in stormy weather. We were alone and I asked for a drink of water; she stood up and went to the washbasin. I noticed some documents with my name on them in the open drawer and tried to read it. She turned, realized what I was trying to do and shut the drawer firmly. A voice immediately followed from the other room: 'What's going on?'

'He tried to read that document,' she said, blushing.

'Did he manage to?'

'No, I noticed it in time.'

'You filth!' screamed the Gestapo man and sized me down so much that I wondered why he did not simply hit me instead.

The meeting between my six interrogators soon finished and they brought me back to the interrogation room. I was expecting another round of questions but one of them stood up and started reading: 'Interrogated Alois Siska ... is charged according para ST. GB 91a of the Third Reich Penal Code that he during the years of 1939 to 1942 betrayed his country, committed acts of espionage and raised arms against Hitler and the Third Reich through escaping from the occupied territory of Bohemia and Moravia, and was caught armed in Germany. Therefore ...'

It was obvious that each cited offence was punishable by death by hanging. So they are going to hang me, I thought. I escaped the sea, only to be killed by people.

It was the sort of surprise I expected least.

Before the shock wore off, they took me back downstairs and sat me on the same small bench as before. I reread the farewell message. Somebody had written it for me after all.

It was already getting dark when they threw us out of the Black Maria into the courtyard of Pankrac prison and took me back to the same cell. As soon as the door closed my fellow prisoners wanted to know everything about my interrogation. I described the proceedings as best I could under the circumstances when the door suddenly opened and somebody dragged me out by the collar. If there hadn't been a balustrade I would have fallen all the way down.

'What did you tell them? Who let you in there?'

They shoved me into a different cell.

Eight days later they drove all us airmen through the blackened streets of Prague. a journey that took longer than the one to the Petschka Palace; we were obviously going somewhere else. We stopped on a slope in a tiny dark alley and they led us along a corridor by torchlight. The door of a cellar slammed behind us ...

Slowly we adjusted to the dim light from a small gas lamp on the wall. Under it was a single bunk about 2 metres long. A small barred window probably led into some yard with a wall at the far end.

A peel of bells interrupted our thoughts. We were somewhere close to the famous Loreta Monastery.

At first we quite liked the bells as they reminded us of Prague in the old days, but after a few days they sounded more like a death knell, which was quite fitting as we were barely alive. A concrete cellar, hundreds of hungry cockroaches, once a day some sort of liquid, which passed for soup, and once a day a ten-minute stretch in a tiny courtyard. We grew restless, argumentative and eventually just apathetic.

The Loreta bells carried on regardless ...

Chapter 21

Whatever Next?

In September 1944 they brought us out, one by one. We thought we were going to be executed. After the time spent in that hellhole we were so demoralized that we did not dare to expect anything else.

Our hopes were raised when we again found ourselves together in the back of a Black Maria. We were taken to the station and put on a train. Our stay in Prague hadn't been the happiest one but we still felt sorry leaving.

We disembarked at some local railway station about 70 kilometres west of Dresden. A massive old castle behind a tall wall did not inspire much confidence in our future. They searched us thoroughly and, under a heavy guard, took us inside.

Our first visitor was Cestmir Chaloupka, a Czech, otherwise known as Ceko, who told us that we had arrived at Colditz Castle, a camp for special prisoners. Chaloupka, a tall, dark, fighter pilot, whose plane had been hit over France, had managed to get to the Channel but had crashed into the sea where the Germans picked him up. He escaped from an ordinary prison camp, was caught and brought to Colditz.

In Colditz, there were three groups of prisoners.

The first were the Prominente first class who were English officers from important families, for example a cousin of the King George VI, Churchill's nephew, the son of General Alexander, and others. They lived in a separate wing and were held as hostages by the Nazi Party.

The second group were the Prominente second class who were those considered to be war criminals by the Nazis. This was us, the

Czechs, members of the RAF. We too were separated from other prisoners and kept under constant guard.

The third and largest group were Allied officers of various arms and ranks. They were kept here as a punishment for escaping from POW camps.

Among them was the famous English fighter pilot Douglas Bader who had lost both his legs. At one time he also led the Czechoslovak 310 Squadron during the Battle of Britain as a part of the famous Duxford Wing.

On 9 August 1941 he collided with a Me 109 over France. He managed to jump out of his damaged Spitfire, but one of his artificial legs remained trapped inside the plane. He was captured and taken to the hospital in St Omer. Surprised Germans brought his artificial leg back. Bader escaped from the hospital but was caught. After a while his fellow pilots dropped him a yellow box with a new leg during an operation. That proved too much for the Germans so they locked him up in the fortress.

There were also a few of those who had escaped from Stalag Luft III at Sagan through the tunnel, described in Paul Brickhill's book, *The Great Escape*. About 800 POWs took part in digging the tunnel for almost a year; it was 150 metres long and up to 3 metres below ground.

The hard work this project represented is difficult to imagine, as well as the danger of being trapped by collapsing earth and the logistical nightmare of disposing of so much earth around the camp! On the top of that it was necessary to make suitable outfits and produce false documents.

The escape through the tunnel took place during the night of 24 March 1944, but it was not until five in the afternoon of the next day that the Germans sounded the alarm. Seventy-six Allied airmen had managed to escape by then, amongst them three Czechs: Arnost Valenta, Bedrich Dvorak and Ivo Tondr.

Eight days later the Senior British Officer (SBO) at Sagan was summoned to the German Camp Commandant and informed: 'Fifty POWs who escaped through the tunnel on the night of 24 March 1944, from the POW camp Stalag Luft III, were caught and shot for resisting arrest and trying to escape again.'

The truth was somewhat different – the Germans locked up the unfortunate ones, took them out in groups and shot them dead. After the war a memorial service was held for those fifty. When the priest read the list of names it included five short words: Pilot Officer Arnost Valenta, Czechoslovak.

Another officer held in Colditz was General Tadeusz Bor-Komorowski who led the Warsaw uprising in the summer of 1944. He was of small build with sparkling eyes and strict manners.

There were also several French generals who opposed the capitulation of their country, one American general and number of Yugoslav, Belgian and Dutch officers. Orderlies and cooks were recruited from mainly English prisoners and they cooked the same food for everybody. Every day we faced turnip soup, ersatz coffee and a sticky brick which passed for bread and was meant to feed ten of us for a whole day. The Germans were scraping the bottom of the barrel and made sure we felt it too. We no longer received Red Cross parcels as the Germans claimed Allied bombing had destroyed them.

We were glad to be amongst British prisoners as it gave us a feeling of safety. Though being labelled 'war criminals' separate accommodation and round-the-clock surveillance were rather ominous. It certainly kept us fearful, not just for our own fate, but also for our loved ones back at home.

This was hardly surprising when the Germans were capable of shooting fifty airmen just for escaping from a POW camp, though to try and escape the enemy was the duty of every soldier.

We kept reminding ourselves that apart from Arnost Valenta all the others were British. So what chance did we have as Czechs charged with committing high treason?

We kept demanding our right of appeal to the Highest Military Court at Torgau, which was chaired by Admiral Bastian. The SBO and one of the prisoners, who was a lawyer, supported our efforts and the Germans eventually allowed us to prepare our defence. Through the organization called Protecting Power and the Red Cross we were assigned a defence layer, a certain Doctor Neumann, a public notary from Colditz. He first came to see us on Monday, 25 September when he asked for our power of attorney and read our defence.

'But my dear men, this is a bit much!'

We knew that so we waited.

'I have got your power of attorney so I will submit your appeal at the Highest Court. But in case of Mister Alois Siska the charge of espionage is proven because unlike the rest of you, he left the occupied country after the outbreak of war.'

Silence fell and my mind was racing. True, we were all in serious trouble but, of course, I was slightly worse off.

I let out my tensions.

'Well, if they hang us, they will have to shoot me as well. At least it will cost them an extra bullet.'

Doctor Neumann smiled and left. We never saw him again and all our demands for him to come and see us were in vain.

Frequent visits from the representatives of various organizations corresponded with the unorthodox mix of prisoners. Nevertheless each time we spotted a plain-clothed person crossing the yard, our doubts grew.

But nobody ever came to see us Czechs again. We were just told that should our appeal be heard, we would be assigned a German defence lawyer at the court.

In fact, they only confirmed our death sentence. Our fate was sealed.

One question remained. When?

Winter was approaching and with it the worst time for my injured legs. I felt it particularly badly in the fortress.

They moved me to the sick bay. In the adjoining room lived Captain Dickie, the English doctor who had tried to protect me from Doctor Jung back in the transit camp near Kassel. His care and news from both fronts were the two things that kept me going, despite my grim prospects for the future.

We even had our own radio – clandestine of course. English naval radio operators had built it with parts supplied by German guards. It was Ceko who organized the smuggling in of the parts – he found a suitable target amongst the guards and waited. At the right moment he threw a cigarette leftover in front of the unsuspecting guard. The German, a strong smoker, came nearer and got so nervous that he started shaking. He went past the cigarette end and looked around, then he picked it up and pulled on it so hard that his eyes watered.

Out of the blue, Ceko stood in front of him. The pleasure of a quick smoke was gone, the guard trembled and hesitated a bit, but he took the offered packet anyway. The fear of the Russian Front was strong at that time. Having taken the bribe, the guard now had to deliver.

There were still some who would not succumb, still believing that Hitler had some other secret weapon beside V-1s and V-2s.

The food rations were reduced even further. Prisoners who suffered with gastroenteritis – I was one of them – were not keen on the usual unappetizing fare. It was worse for the healthy ones who descended on the wooden barrel containing the kitchen waste like vultures, and with their bare hands tried to fish out even the tiniest piece of rotten turnip skin which the cooks had discarded. Nobody took any notice of rank or status – there wasn't time. You had to be quick before the Germans took the barrel to the nearby pig farm.

Often the lucky one who had painstakingly cleared the few precious scraps with his own toothbrush and added them to his soup, received a kick up the backside or a rifle butt from the guards for his efforts.

It was said that it was impossible to escape from Colditz but they kept counting us nonetheless, with the main roll calls at seven in the morning and five in the afternoon. The Germans were usually punctual and our British colonel was also a stickler for timekeeping. He was a well-built, grey-haired Scot, always immaculately turned out in a full Scottish uniform, whatever the circumstances.

When the ten-deep rows of prisoners were ready for counting, he used to walk in front of them, hands behind his back. When the hour struck, he called, 'Gentlemen, please.'

Simultaneously the keys turned in the big gates and a German officer stormed into the courtyard, followed by his sidekicks and a horde of armed soldiers with dogs. He took the appelle and the SBO would call out, 'Thank you, gentlemen.'

This meant we could stand at ease. The rows started moving and the formation was broken as the Germans, one in the front and one in the back, tried to count.

One morning, while I was still capable of attending the roll call, the SBO called out at the usual time, 'Gentlemen, please.'

He waited. A minute passed but no Germans. He ordered us to stand at ease and kept walking. The Germans turned up several minutes later.

The SBO saluted the German officer and continued his walk.

'What's all this about? Why don't you call them to attention?'

'I called them at 0700 hrs as you ordered. Now it's four minutes past seven. I will call the next roll call at 1700 hrs – according to your orders.'

'Boo ... boo ...' the prisoners jeered, the rows moving.

The Germans could not count us and the Nazi shouted, 'Stand to attention or we will shoot!'

They didn't.

They managed to count us by midday but only with the help of the dogs.

One night we were woken up by a commotion. They brought in several hundred French officers whom they had evacuated from somewhere on the Eastern Front. They were in a pretty poor shape as they had marched for miles without any shoes, and their feet were swollen and badly grazed. A few days later they marched them on. Was the same fate awaiting us?

Christmas arrived. We did not expect any miracles, but we firmly believed it would be the last of its kind. We put together in groups the last leftovers of any parcels to make a Christmas cake. We hardly had any cigarettes left.

The orderly in the sickbay, nicknamed Joe, knew that I did not enjoy smoking any more, which was not surprising after all those pills I'd had to take! I left him my cigarette ration.

'Joe, if you'd like them, take them, please.'

He thanked me and left, but came back a few minutes later with some Ceylon tea and a piece of paper with a message in pencil written on it: 'Please pay Mr A. Siska the sum of fifteen pounds. Signed: Lord Lascelles.'

I did not know whether I should take it as a joke, but I put the paper in my pocket anyway.

New Year 1945 came and both fronts were closing in on each other. The end of the war was inevitable.

New Year in Colditz did not start well. The American General had his death sentence confirmed. He had ninety days left. When would it be our turn?

At the end of March, at one o'clock in the morning, a German officer stormed in with the usual horde of armed soldiers and dogs, and ordered all the Prominente to assemble, apparently for evacuation.

Our Scottish SBO refused to let them be separated. They argued for hours. In the end the German shouted, 'I will shoot if I have to!'

'Over my dead body,' replied the composed man in tartan trousers. I found that Scots were always brave.

The German gave up but we had very little to cheer about. From the news we gleaned from our secret radio, we knew that the end of fascism was close but we had no idea about the intentions of the fanatics, and there were quite a few amongst our guards.

We were thankful for each day we survived ...

Chapter 22

Days of Freedom

A few days after the unsuccessful German attempt to evacuate us from Colditz I was ordered to get ready to leave – without any luggage. The German guard assured me in the presence of the SBO and other British officers that I would come to no harm. Even so I said my goodbyes to everyone.

Two guards escorted me to the field hospital attached to a POW camp nearby, apparently so that I could be called before a repatriation committee. We just could not make the Germans out.

The next morning I could not believe my eyes when I was greeted by the sight of trees and green grass, the smell of spring and birds singing. Prisoners were wandering freely by a pond outside, with no high wall or barbed wire in sight. The view stretched well into the fields beyond ...

There was a large room with a balcony in the former sanatorium, inside which there were about 200 badly wounded Allied prisoners, some POWs from as far back as the Crete campaign of 1941 and even Dunkirk. Everybody was waiting for the decision of the committee. The delay made my German guards very nervous, as they did not know whether to wait with me for the committee's decision or leave me there.

At the intervention of the English doctor, Major Frosby, the local German officer in charge took responsibility for me and dismissed the guards.

I can hardly describe my feelings. One can appreciate freedom fully, not when one loses it, but when one cannot get it back. Or when one gets it back.

I wandered further but whereas none of the German guards took any notice, I could barely believe it. After all, the place was full of cripples, so who would run away? And where to?

Some 200 metres away stood a white building, which turned out to be a female agricultural college. There wasn't barbed wire around their compound either, just the sign: 'NO ENTRY!'

By day the war didn't exist; only at night could we hear distant gunfire. We were cut off from the rest of the world, without any supplies. The guards were in contact with no one.

One morning the schoolgirls left their school and they headed across the fields with rucksacks on their backs. The next day the guardroom was busy – the soldiers were packing up. Then they too left on their bicycles, heading west. They could have taken the main road but they chose to plod across the fields. They must have had their reasons.

The only one left was the Sergeant in charge of the guards. He had an injured arm and an Iron Cross, and moved upstairs to where the widowed lady owner lived. The war was obviously over for him.

Later that day a German field kitchen came in with five men and positioned themselves close to the building.

We heard an aircraft and later spotted it circling the nearby airfield. It kept reappearing and each time came nearer the field hospital. As soon as it disappeared from view we heard machine-gun fire.

I pointed out to Major Frosby that it could be a lone wolf so we asked the field kitchen squad to leave the compound. The young and frightened Germans moved across the main road to the edge of the wood, but their peace did not last long. The plane returned, clearly showing the Allied marking of a white star on its fuselage and attacked the field kitchen. Then it circled around once more and vanished. We waited for a while in case it came back, but eventually I got several walking wounded together and headed for the field kitchen. It took us a long time.

The Germans were nowhere to be seen and the plane had made quite a mess of the place. There were broken boxes everywhere, bread, tins and a few broken wine bottles scattered on the ground.

'Look at all that nosh.'

'Watch out! The Germans are coming back!'

We hesitated for a split second. In front of us were five Germans and a field kitchen full of food, while behind us was a field hospital full of starving people. And that plane could easily come back.

'Let's arrest them!' I shouted and grabbed one of the rifles which the Germans had left inside the lorry.

We did not have to even aim at them – they approached us with their hands up. They made no protest and were just glad it was all over. We took them and their papers back to the hospital.

We brought the food into the main hall of the sanatorium and distributed it amongst the hungry prisoners – it was an unexpected and welcome surprise. We locked up the Germans in a small room under guard.

Meanwhile, we had to get ready for the fast approaching front. I took over the empty guardroom with a few able-bodied prisoners.

With darkness gathering the noise of gunfire grew stronger, and it got even worse during the night. Shrapnel landed on the roof and we could see numerous flashes which frightened some of the wounded lying on the balcony just below the roof. We had to move them down to the cellar.

The indoor water pump kicked off suddenly. The sound of water filling the tank was too much for some and one of the men started shouting that the Germans were going to poison us with gas. He needed medication to calm him down.

It was well after midnight and the noise outside continued. The owner of the sanatorium rushed into the guardroom with a small child in her arms. The child was screaming and shaking as the mother implored us, 'Please, please do something ...'

What could we do? We were all in the same boat. So we made space for her in the guardroom.

The next morning found us all exhausted and suffering from a lack of sleep. It was quiet outside – only distant gunfire could still be heard. A large Alsatian was hiding by the door. He came to me. Not long ago he would have torn me apart, but now he wanted comforting. I stroked his head. There was debris everywhere but the spring morning was beautiful.

Shortly after nine o'clock we heard a roar interspersed by machine-gun fire. Suddenly an armoured personnel carrier appeared on the main road, followed by tanks, one after another, all with white stars of the Allies instead of the German black crosses. They went past firing their machine guns continuously down both sides of the road.

What should we do? They were going straight past us without knowing we were there. We had to grab their attention somehow, so an American prisoner and I took a bed sheet and walked towards the column of tanks.

They were still going past, though we were only a short distance away. Suddenly one of them stopped and slowly turned towards us. It kept on coming at us, with all its guns aimed on us. We stiffened ...

I'd never before faced a moving tank. My grey uniform, I thought, will they think that I am a German?

The tank clanked to a halt right in front of us. A voice called from the open hatch, 'Who are you?'

I can't remember who answered him first but I don't think it was me.

After that it was easy. The tank crew called for medical help and within two hours their tents were erected in the grounds of our sanatorium. We all received medical treatment and were given food and drink.

The Germans prisoners were taken away by the military police who did not waste any time on them. Their commanding officer had to go too – lodging with the widow had not saved him.

Within a few hours the Americans had set up a cinema and we were watching films – the latest news followed by some hilarious comedy. We could not follow the dialogue very well as the gunfire kept interrupting.

The front was still all around us. Transport vehicles of emaciated but free prisoners of war of all kinds and nationalities were filling the roads. They all were very happy people now but their appearance spoke of the suffering they had endured.

It took another fortnight before they could evacuate us safely to Erfurt and from there, after a few more days, by plane to Brussels. At last we really were free and well looked after.

We arrived in Belgium on 5 May 1945 and three days later Germany capitulated. There was music playing everywhere from early morning and people embraced, their joy knowing no bounds. The whole town was covered with flags and flowers.

I felt very sad. I was longing for some news from home and at the same time I was afraid of what I might hear. And my legs! While a prisoner surrounded by so many injured comrades and often in a confined space, I had not felt so aware of my problem, but now

141

with a new life ahead of me I was still dependent on the help of strangers ...

After some rest, numerous medical examinations and necessary delousing we were given new uniforms and flown back to England. At Manston we all received a new identity card and some pocket money. They also wished me a happy birthday, as it was Tuesday, 15 May – I was thirty-one years old and had forgotten all about it.

After more than three years I was back in England.

And the English? They were still composed and decisive, but tired out.

The next day they organized a special train, which took us through London to Wolverhampton. The names of the railway stations were readable again but many houses and even whole parts of towns, especially London, were in ruins. Destruction was visible everywhere.

As a Czech looking in I wondered what the English would say to that and discovered that the general attitude was: 'We won the war anyway.'

Yes, they did. And they had always felt that they would win the war even if they lost some battles. An ambulance took me back to Cosford where I had first joined the RAF back in 1940. There I found out that Colditz had been liberated on 16 April just a few hours after I had left. The German officer who had failed in his plan to evacuate the Prominente was captured. It was apparently intended that all Prominente, including the Czechs, would have been handed over in Bavaria and at Hitler's orders shot dead.

I also found out about the fate of the rest of my crew: Josef Scerba had been repatriated; Pavel Svoboda managed to escape from the POW camp at Lammsdorf, got back to the occupied homeland and later joined a partisan group in Moravia.

I wondered why we were not executed after being sentenced by the Gestapo, especially as the Torgau military court did not usually waste much time over the confirmation of such a sentence. Only later did I hear that Churchill had threatened that for each prisoner wearing a British uniform shot by the Germans, two German prisoners of a higher rank would be shot as a reprisal. So the life of Arnost Valenta, one of the organizers of the Great Escape from Sagan, was not sacrificed for nothing. Within two years all those

Germans involved in these murders had been executed by the Allies.

I was moved from Cosford to the Queen Victoria Hospital at East Grinstead in Sussex, where Allied doctors led by Sir Archibald McIndoe tried their best to restore the health of burned and frost-bitten airmen. For many there was no chance of regaining their former face or missing limbs.

On my way there I had to stop at a bank to sort out my overdue pay. Out of curiosity I showed the bank clerk the slip of paper with Lord Lascelles' signature, which I had kept as a souvenir. The clerk took it away and a few moments later he returned saying that the sum had been credited to my account ...

One day I had a visitor but I could not recognize his face as he looked the same as so many other burned airmen – fresh scars on his chin and neck, no earlobes, new eyebrows, no eyelashes, one eye half closed, nose of out place and the whole face covered in blotches of various shades, pointing to the age of numerous skin transplants. On his tunic were three Czechoslovak Military Crosses, three Medals for Bravery and many others.

After a few months in the hospital I was used to accepting every-body's appearance as they were, without any embarrassment. On top of that Sister Mary would not allow for any shyness. Before one visitor reached my bedside, she introduced us. 'Good morning, Mister Siska, this is Mister Truhlar who wanted to see you. Well, gentlemen, I shall leave you to it. I am sure you have a lot to talk about.'

I stretched out my hand but he hesitated before offered his in return – mere bones covered in fresh pink skin. Only his smile put me on the right track.

'I had some transplants done on my legs.' I said, almost as an apology.

Truhlar had several done to him – after his first crash. He was a rear gunner on a Wimpy. Back in September 1940 his plane was returning from a bombing raid and because the radio had been damaged, they found themselves in a balloon barrage over London and crashed. Truhlar's turret broke away from the burning fuselage on impact and landed some distance away from the rest of the plane. He was the only survivor, but was badly burned.

The scars remained and, perhaps even stronger, his love of flying. He retrained as a pilot and transferred to a fighter squadron.

In June 1944 he was shot down again, his legs were badly broken and he was burned again – mainly his face and hands ...

By July 1946 my legs were not responding to their first major operation so they had to operate on my spinal nerves, which meant another long spell in bed.

I received my first letter from home. It was from my brother; my mother was still in hospital. I also received a reply from Coastal Command describing their efforts to find us in the North Sea. Sergeant Palmer, whom I had met in Holland at the beginning of 1942, was obviously right – a lack of fuel and worsening weather prevented our rescue.

Franta Truhlar came to say goodbye, as he was being sent home. I wanted to go with him. He was returning with a renewed will to live and went on to serve on Spitfires at Prague Kbely airfield. He came from a little place called Lomnice nad Popelkou. One day he was going home on the train with another ex-pilot, Gusta Kopal when a young mother with a small girl came into their compartment, the child stared at his burned face and she started crying.

'Why are you crying and what are you staring at?' the mother enquired. Only then did she notice his face. 'This is awful! Such people should not be allowed to move freely in public ... can't you see you scared her?'

Both airmen left the compartment; Franta's eyes were welling up.

'Will I look like this for the rest of my life?'

Gusta tried to comfort him but it did not work, so he went back to the compartment and collected their luggage.

Franta became a recluse after that ...

At the end of 1946, while I was still in hospital, Doctor Archibald McIndoe came to see me and said, 'I've just had some bad news. Major Truhlar had an accident on 3 December. His plane hit the ground near his birthplace. I don't know ... do you think it was just an accident?'

I did not know so I did not answer. We sat in silence for a while and then he left. The badly injured needed him ...

PART THREE

Chapter 23

Until the Bitter End

By the end of March 1947 I was due to return home on leave from post-war England. I would be discharged from the hospital at East Grinstead where I had spent twenty-three months recovering from my many operations, two of them very serious. My legs had suffered badly from frostbite and the subsequent gangrene so I was given five million units of penicillin, just in case of infection, as at that time penicillin was not readily available in my country. By now I was a fully-fledged member of the Guinea Pig Club.

The plastic surgeons in this famous hospital did a marvellous job. Before they started on me, I had spent several months confined to bed and five years either in a wheelchair or on crutches. After they finished with me I could walk slowly and with considerable pain, but I only needed one walking stick. For that I am eternally grateful.

In my discharge papers addressed to the Czechoslovak authorities, it said amongst other things: 'Further operations will be needed on his left leg, together with a local skin transplant on both heels. We therefore request that this patient is allowed to return to our ward at the end of his leave for further treatment.' In addition to the usual travel papers I also received a special repatriation document in Russian, which I needed for the Soviet authorities in Germany. I refused the free air ticket as I wished to travel overland to see the aftermath of the war.

I left Victoria Station for Dover and continued across the Channel to Calais. I spent the crossing in the bar with some British soldiers drinking whisky so I did not even notice the rough sea and the cliffs of Dover disappearing in the distance. A fast French train took me to Gare d'Nord in Paris. The next day I left from Gare d'Ost via Germany to the Czech town of Cheb, where memories of my first flying school came flooding back.

The view from the train was shocking. As a former bomber pilot I could not help feeling somewhat responsible ... but the will to rebuild and create a new and better life was clearly visible.

On my return to Prague I lodged at the Airmen's House at Vladislavova Street and next morning visited the medical council of the Ministry of Defence. Its chairman, an army doctor called Colonel Bergman, read my medical reports and said, 'You will take some leave and have spa treatment to help you recover.'

I interrupted him. 'With due respect, sir, I do not want to see another bed! A white sheet to me is like a red rag to a bull. I want to get on!'

'Very well. Report to the Squadron at Kbely – they will know what to do with you,' he added and dismissed me.

The Commanding Officer at Kbely was Lieutenant Colonel Secky – another ex-RAF pilot. Together with my documents, I also handed over to him a receipt for my personal belongings, which consisted of two large, white, locked service bags containing my new battledress, two blue shirts, a pistol and some cigarettes and chocolate. He took a bundle of keys from his desk and we went to the storeroom. My bags were there, but had been cut open and were empty.

'Take your pick,' he said and pointed to the floor covered in various bits and pieces. I did not find many of my belongings and I missed most of all the two shirts, as they were difficult to come by. I only had one so I had to wash it every other day.

I was given a month's leave which I spent mainly in Moravia. It was fantastic to be back home after seven long years ... my mother was ecstatic. She had prayed for my safe return and had always believed that I would come back one day.

The month went by quickly and on my return to the Squadron I was appointed Adjutant. I was somewhat perplexed by the fact that all my fellow ex-RAFs were flying again already and had been promoted by two ranks. I was still only a Flying Officer.

I went to see the personnel officer at the Air Force HQ, who told me that I had spent too long in England after the war. When they reactivated and promoted all the others, I had been forgotten. Now it was too late ...

I had one more ace up my sleeve in the form of a document from the Czechoslovak Embassy in London, according to which I should be given a car in lieu of the one I had lost after being shot down. When I submitted this document to the officer in charge of vehicles at the Ministry I was told that I should have claimed that immediately after the war and not two years later as everything had gone ...

At the end of the summer of 1947 I was transferred to the military airfield of Vysoke Myto-Kujebina where the Commanding Officer was Colonel Dolezel. The Squadron Commander was Flight Lieutenant Vaclav Svec and his second in command was Flying Officer Bedrich Kruzik – both ex-RAF. Kruzik and I were single so we stayed in a local hotel.

Came the autumn, the time of the traditional country feasts, and a local farmer invited Svec and myself for Sunday lunch. We knew that some spirits would be served in the course of it. We also knew that it was likely to be of a dubious quality as there was a shortage of any decent spirits on the market at that time. So we asked the lady of the house for a tablespoon of warm goose dripping. This background knowledge of my colleague served us well – there were numerous toasts, which left many guests feeling not their best. Only the two of us – thanks to that goose dripping – survived.

When I received confirmation from the Institute of Air Medicine that I was only considered well enough to fly single-engine planes, I asked for a reassessment and was posted back to Kbely where I joined other applicants. The evaluation was done on a C-106, reminding me of my first pilot training in Cheb in 1936. I could not have forgotten that much as I passed after only two weeks.

One of the other applicants was a certain Lieutenant Colonel Dobrichovsky of an early warning unit of the Ministry of Defence. He came up to me one day, and said, 'I have been waiting for you. Have you ever thought of joining my unit?'

'Sir, that's out of the question. I have to go back Kujebina as ordered,' I replied as politely as I could.

Back at Kujebina I was flying C-106s, together with Svec, a former wireless operator with 311 Squadron, and Kruzik, a former navigator with 68 Squadron.

The political situation in the country was getting hotter and the number of newly established branches of the Communist Party in factories and offices grew by the day. Despite that and the frequent sessions of the Central Committee of the Communist Party, there was no sign of things to come, perhaps with the exception of the recruitment methods of new party members. My turn came soon enough. One Monday morning when I unlocked my desk I found a copy of the application form for party membership in my drawer. I went mad!

'Choulik!' I shouted into the corridor and waited for the duty officer to appear. 'Who put this here?' I asked angrily pointing at the form. He lifted his glasses and denied any knowledge of it.

'Take it away and destroy it!' I ordered angrily.

This spectacle was repeated the following Monday. After these two attempts the form stopped appearing but rumours about my refusal started to circulate.

The beginning of Lent was the ball season, and after all the years of war, captivity and convalescence this was my first chance to attend such a social occasion. The ball lasted all night, but it was to be my last.

After the Communist coup in February 1948 I was transferred to the Air Force Academy at Hradec Kralove. The reason was simple. All ex-RAFs who had English wives were discharged. Amongst them was Flight Lieutenant Zdenek Sychrovsky who until then had been in charge of the School of Night Vision. As I too had qualified at this school back in England, I became his second in command. The new commander of the academy was General Frantisek Rypl, also ex-RAF, but by now a Communist Party member.

I was subsequently put in charge of the School of Night Vision, together with taking charge of flight simulators, and made a professor of tactical flying. My second in command on the flight simulators was Lieutenant Prochazka, chairman of the company's Communist Party branch. My two colleagues were Flying Officer Brand and Lieutenant Havlicek, who became the mechanic.

The room for the simulators was allocated and made ready, as we were expecting them any day. Six simulators were bought from England for thirty-six million Czechoslovak crowns – a lot of money. Four were meant for us at the Academy and two for the advanced course at the airfield in Pardubice. The Commanding Officer there was another ex-RAF, former fighter pilot Flight Lieutenant Zdenek Skarvada.

There were several other ex-RAFs there: Major Macenauer, a former navigator, Flight Lieutenant Josef Scerba, former wireless operator and member of my KX-B crew with 311 Squadron, Flight Lieutenant Keprt, fighter pilot, and Flight Lieutenant Lastovka, another ex-navigator. There was also an armourer, Flight Lieutenant Vacek.

One day I was passing some aircraftmen digging a trench. They were stripped to the waist and without their caps, but when I got nearer they all stopped working and stood to attention. I returned the salute and enquired about the progress of their work on a hot day. Then I carried on as they quickly returned to their digging.

I had only gone a few yards when I overheard: 'Comrades, you did not acknowledge me, a major, but you did acknowledge that flying officer. I will have you punished!' It was Major Krugler, the main political officer at the Academy.

'We did not see you, sir,' came the reply.

At the next officers' meeting Major Krugler dwelt on this incident and threatened to punish anybody who did not behave as he demanded ...

At last the simulators were installed. After they had been checked, the training started in earnest. Most attendees welcomed the simulators, but there were a few who considered them unnecessary.

In July I went the Trencianske Teplice Spa in Slovakia for further treatment. The head of the military sanatorium was Colonel Baxa. During my first week there I met Miss Vlasta Prochazkova who quickly became my constant companion. A week later we had just returned from a walk and went to our rooms to get ready for dinner. Much to my surprise my room was unlocked and inside I found a captain from OBZ. He closed the door behind me, leant on it and said, 'Comrade Flying Officer Siska, you are under arrest and are to come with me to Prague immediately!'

I was in love, which was why I did not grasp the danger of my new situation.

'Is this some sort of a joke?' I asked.

'Here is the warrant for your arrest,' he replied and showed me some document.

I read it and retorted, 'I was arrested before, imprisoned by the Gestapo but at least they gave me something to eat.'

The Captain, still leaning on the door, demanded my assurance that I would return after dinner and only let me out after I'd done so.

I always greeted the ladies sitting on either side of my table in the dining room, but on this occasion they did not acknowledge my greetings.

When I was finishing my dinner, the waiter brought me a message that Colonel Baxa wished to see me so I went to the top table.

'Don't worry. It'll be all right,' said the Colonel and shook my hand.

The Captain was furious. Because of my delayed return we had missed our train and the next one did not leave until midnight. I suggested that we retire to the bar. I chose not to tell him that I was meeting Miss Prochazkova there. He hesitated for a while but eventually agreed on the condition that I would not discuss my arrest with anybody.

During a dance a stranger whispered in my ear, 'Beware, they are after you.' I could only assume that the whole spa already knew about my arrest.

When paying the bill, I suddenly remembered that I had about thirty English pounds in my pocket, which would not be a lot of use where I was going. I had to get rid of them quickly so asked my minder if I could return a book to Miss Prochazkova. He agreed.

Back in my room I took a book out and showed it to him. Out in the corridor, I put the pounds inside and handed it over to Miss Prochazkova. We quickly kissed good-bye ...

When I enquired what I should take with me, the Captain said that I would not need anything any more ... up until then he had been reasonably friendly but at the station his behaviour changed – he locked me in the compartment and stood guard outside. I wondered in vain where I had gone wrong and fell asleep ...

It was raining in Prague. We went to Stefanik Barracks at Smichov where my minder took me to the Fifth Department (OBZ). Inside I met my old friends from England – Flight Lieutenant Smrcka and Flying Officer Prokop.

'What's the hell is going on? Why have I been arrested?' I asked instead of greeting them.

'We have no idea and the boss has got the papers locked up in his safe,' said Smrcka. 'He was summoned to the procurator – he'll be back about ten.'

'Fine, so I'll go and have something to eat. I haven't eaten since last night,' I declared and headed for the door. Not so. My minder informed me that I was not allowed to leave the room. Some plain-clothed person then asked me to go next door to be interrogated.

I sat down in a chair and lifted my legs painfully onto the edge of the table next to the typist's desk, apologizing to her as I did so. The interrogation started. When they repeated the same question about my last meeting with General Janousek, I took my legs off the table, pulled the sheet of paper out of the typewriter and threw it at the interrogator, saying, 'I do not answer stupid questions twice!'

The door opened and a stocky man walked in. My interrogator stood to attention and reported that I was being difficult.

The new arrival did not bother introducing himself and started shouting, 'Trial! Prison for you!'

I faced him down.

'Who do you think you're shouting at? Where were you when the war was on? Doesn't this mean anything to you?' I pointed at my medal ribbons. Then I added, less angrily, 'The door closes on both sides, so just make sure you don't find yourself on the wrong one.'

I don't know whether this made him leave but he did so, slamming the door behind him. I later found that he was actually the head of the Fifth Department. The rest of the interrogation was conducted peacefully.

Back in the first office I found my new minder, this time an air force captain, but also an OBZ. His orders were to take me back to the Fifth Department at the LVA in Hradec Kralove.

As with his predecessor, he was very official and stood guard outside the locked compartment. We reached Hradec at night and in silence arrived at the Hotel Avion.

I broke the silence. 'This is where I'm staying.'

'My orders are to take you to the airfield,' he protested.

'That's all very well, but there isn't suitable accommodation for officers and on top of that I don't feel well so will sleep here,' I decided. 'You can stay with me – I've got another room,' I offered. After some deliberation we ended up in my hotel apartment.

He stayed in the front room and I bedded down for the night next door. There was no chance of getting any sleep – I was racking my brain for the reason for my arrest.

After a while he knocked on my door. 'I have to go the airfield. Give me your word that you will not disappear.'

'My medical condition doesn't allow me to,' I said. We then agreed that he would bring me my return travel permit by nine o'clock the next morning. I showed him out of the hotel and locked the front door.

Alone at last! I locked myself in my room and checked that nobody had tampered with my briefcase full of documents. I took out my passport, which, according to the post-February directive, I should hand over to that same Fifth Department. Paranoia had set in and the communists suspected everybody who had fought on the western front would try to escape.

I tore my passport to bits and burned it in a stove in the kitchen. It was the only thing which worried me, and having dealt with it, I fell asleep happily ...

I had my breakfast in the hotel as normal and when nobody turned up by nine o'clock, I took the bus to the local prosecution office. The prosecutor, also an ex-RAF, greeted me and enquired why I was there. When I explained everything he concluded that there was nothing he could do, as he hadn't yet received any written report. At my insistence he telephoned the prosecutor back in Prague who had signed my release the day before. He must have got proof over the telephone as he smiled at me and let me go back to the spa.

'They haven't delivered the necessary travel permit. I've just got enough time to catch the last direct train but I'm not buying a ticket,' I muttered on my departure ...

I found a seat on the train, opened the window and watched the stationmaster getting ready to signal for the train to depart. At that moment a corporal with red cord on his shoulders ran onto the platform waving a piece of paper in his hand – my travel permit. The train was already moving when I snatched it from his hand ...

Back in the sanatorium Dr Baxa welcomed me very cordially indeed. No less cordial was my reunion with Vlasta Prochazkova. We all had a lot to talk about.

The rest of my stay at the spa went without incident, though twice an officer came all the way from Prague to check on me.

The training programme at the Academy was in full swing. I wanted to buy a bicycle to cover the distance between the lecture rooms and the training area and discovered I was entitled to a special voucher for one which I had to get from the local council office. When I went there to ask for it, I also put my name down – as a war veteran – for a flat. The clerk asked, 'Which front did you fight on, Comrade?'

'As an airman I was on the western one,' I replied.

'In that case we have not got any flats available. But of course if you were on the eastern front there would be one available immediately,' he added for explanation.

At the end of the year I was summoned to the deputy commander's office, one Lieutenant Colonel Hurych. He pushed some paper towards me and said, 'Sign it!'

'I'll need to read it first, sir,' I said.

'It's a reward for your contribution to the reconstruction of the people's air force. Don't tell anybody – you're the only one who's got it. And you are not even a Party member ... and you fought on the western front!' he said somewhat apologetically. I did not argue, signed on the dotted line and received 900 crowns.

I also received some very sad news: my future father-in-law, General Jan Prochazka, had died. When I saw him for the last time in the military hospital in Prague, he asked me to take good care of his daughter and wife. I would have promised him that even under less emotional circumstances.

[*Translator's note: My late grandfather was born on 21 June 1893 in Vizovice, a small town in Moravia. Before the outbreak of the First World War he was studying Latin and Greek at the Charles University in Prague. As his homeland was part of the Austro-Hungarian Empire he was drafted into the Austrian Army to fight against the Russians. He later joined the newly formed Czechoslovak Legion, fighting with the Russians for a new nation independent of the Austrian hegemony. With the capitulation of Russia at the time of the Revolution in 1917, he was unable to return home westwards. He eventually arrived home with the 8,000-strong Czech Legion intact via Siberia and Canada in 1920.*

As a member of the 9th Infantry Regiment he was stationed in the northern Bohemian town of Most where he met his future wife Miss Vlasta Hlavkova. They moved to Prague and in 1924 my mother, also to be called Vlasta, was born. My grandfather enrolled at the Military Academy in Prague to study infantry tactics. After his graduation he was appointed professor at the same military academy. In between 1937 and 1939 he was the commander of the 4th Group of the Czechoslovak Army stationed in Olomouc.

Once the Germans had occupied all of Czechoslovakia in March 1939, he was discharged from the army, and the family returned to Prague. The officers of the old HQ formed a clandestine resistance group called 'Defence of the Nation'. My grandfather became an active member and, because of his links with Moravia, he often acted as a courier. In November 1940 the group was arrested following a tip-off. My grandfather was taken to the notorious Kounic University Hostel in Brno for interrogation by the Gestapo. From there he was transferred to a German prison in Breslau, and then to Altmoabit prison in Berlin, where he was tried and sentenced to eleven years incarceration by the German Military Court. He was moved to the prison in Bayreuth to start his sentence.

In 1945 he was liberated by the US Third Army and spent the last month of the War as a liaison officer. On returning to Prague he was given command of the 1st Czechoslovak Independent Brigade, which had fought on the eastern front under General Ludvik Svoboda. During 1946 and 1947 he returned to the military academy to resume teaching. From 1947 until his death he was second in command to General Bocek, the Chief of Military Headquarters.

After the Communist coup in February 1948 he was branded an enemy of the state. His health started to deteriorate as a result of his wartime imprisonment, and he was hospitalized. He was kept under arrest in the Prague Military Hospital, sharing a room with General Heliodor Pika. (General Pika was later moved to prison and executed by the Communists). His worsening health required antibiotics, which were not readily available in Czechoslovakia. By this time my father had just spent over two years in Queen Victoria Hospital in East Grinstead in England, and was a member of the Guinea Pig Club. He approached his many friends in the club asking for help. For this he was summoned to the Czech Ministry of Defence's infamous Fifth Department and told, 'It is not in the interest of the country for General Jan Prochazka to survive.' My father was then informed that he could not marry his fiancée Miss Vlasta Prochazkova because of her father's standing.

My grandfather died, still under arrest, in the Military Hospital on 18 December 1948.]

Our Flight Simulator Section (in Czech initials CPK) had a study visit from two Soviet officers. They inspected everything, watched all training sessions closely and took a lot of notes. Later, in the New Year, I was called to the personnel department of the Ministry of Defence where I was told that I had been granted the status of Graduate of the Air Force Academy. It made my day.

Soon afterwards Major Kugler, the chief political officer at the Academy, called me into his office.

'Join the party and you will be promoted immediately to the rank of Major.'

'If I am not good enough as a non-Party member, I would hardly be any better if I joined,' I replied and left. He was not amused. That must have contributed to the next chain of events.

In March 1949 I received a 'Confirmation Document' from the Ministry according to which I was, seemingly at my own request, deactivated. It was a very unpleasant surprise indeed. The only positive moment came during the handover of my post of the head of CPK to Pilot Officer Prochazka, my second in command, who stated seriously, 'We will fight to get you back!'

But with nobody to take charge of the SNV, I locked the door and handed over the keys.

I was sad to leave the Academy, and moved in with my fiancée and her mother in their Prague flat. I was dismissed from the Air Force without any right to renumeration.

I started to look for a job suitable for my health, but I was only allowed to work manually. When I went to the placement committee at the Ministry, General Malec, who was in charge, made it clear.

'You have three choices: mines, foundries or co-operative farms.'

He did not waste time talking to me after that.

Some of my similarly affected friends were trying to get jobs with the principal photographic studio in Prague – the famous Langhans. The manager there was a certain Belak, a former Pilot Officer who had fought on the eastern front with Svoboda's army. He gave me an interview but had no more suitable jobs going, unless I had a clean driving licence, in which case I could be his driver.

'But there is a snag – you are a Flying Officer and I am only a Pilot Officer,' he said.

'Don't take any notice of that,' I replied joyfully. 'I have to earn my living somehow.'

I filled in the job application form, he signed it and said, 'You have to take it personally to our head of personnel. I will ring him so you can come straight back to me.'

To my polite greeting the personnel manager said angrily, 'You Benes outcasts, you traitors, you want better jobs? You are not fit for anything but mines, foundries or farms!' With that he tore up my application form in front of my eyes.

There was no point going back to Mr Belak. I went home where I found both women in tears. The reason was obvious – my fiancée had just been expelled from the university where she was studying Political and Social Sciences a mere term before graduating, because she was marrying a 'western front veteran'. We put our heads together and decided that I would try to see the Minister of Defence, General Svoboda. It was not an easy task in those days but I succeeded. He agreed to see me and when I gave him the full story, he proceeded to lecture me about the difficult political situation in the same manner a lance corporal would speak to new recruits. His office must have been bugged. When he finished, I replied, 'Minister, we are both front-line soldiers. I don't know whether you were wounded, but I was. We both made it back – you are the Minister of Defence and I was thrown out of the Air Force without rights to anything and I cannot even be employed as a driver – so what am I supposed to do? Jump off the bridge?'

Without saying anything, he took one of his business cards and wrote on the back of it: 'To the duty officer at the HQ: Arrange an audience for Flying Officer Siska with the head of the Air Force, Air Commodore Vicherek.' He then signed the front of the card with his beautiful flowing signature. I took it with thanks and left his office.

At the HQ the duty officer personally escorted me to the door of the Air Commodore's office. But before we got there, I had to be vetted by the Fifth Department. It took three attempts before one of their secretaries agreed to talk to me. When I explained the reason for my visit, he exclaimed, 'Siska – we know each other from Plzen! You'll be fine.'

'I never served in Plzen,' I protested.

'So I must know you from somewhere else. Never mind, you can go and see the Air Commodore,' he said.

'Fine, but he wants your approval in writing – you know that,' I insisted.

He swore but wrote something and put it in a sealed envelope. Air Commodore Vicherek read the note and wanted to know the reason for my visit. I described my work at the Air Force Academy and also my discussion with the Minister. At the end I asked, 'Does it mean that because I am not a Party member, I can no longer be in the forces?'

'I will look into it and will let you know in two weeks' time. But don't come back here, come to my flat instead,' he said and handed me his address.

Back at home we went through the events several times and concluded that there wasn't anything else we could do.

Three weeks later I was reinstated at the Academy so I never did make it back to see the Air Commodore. On my return I reported to General Rypl, now head of the Academy. He rubbed his hands in delight.

'Air Commodore Vicherek was here personally. Carry on with your duties as if nothing ever happened.'

First in line was the CPK (Flight Simulator) section, but my office was locked. I asked the duty corporal who had got the keys. Apparently Comrade Pilot Officer Prochazka who was watching the students taking off.

'When he comes back for lunch, tell him I am back and ask him to leave the keys for me,' I told him.

I picked up the rest of the keys from the head office and returned to the Night Vision School where I happily busied myself until lunch.

After lunch I returned to the CPK office only to find the duty corporal waiting for me – not with the required key but with a message from Pilot Officer Prochazka who specifically stated that he did not want me ever to turn up again.

That amounted to insubordination and obstruction of fulfilling my duties, and could only be resolved by the head of the Academy. He listened to my report nervously clasping his hands, then he signed a flight order and said, 'Fly to Pardubice airfield, there is plenty for you to do there.'

I flew myself to Pardubice in a Piper aircraft and arrived just at the end of a pre-flying session for new pilots. Their Commanding Officer, Flight Lieutenant Skarvada, did not waste any time.

'You've arrived just in time. We'll be practising a fly-past for the VE Day celebrations. You will observe the flight above the airfield and we will discuss it afterwards.'

So I went to the take-off area and watched the Me 109s performing the formation flight. There was a lot to watch but hardly any need to discuss the manoeuvre later.

It was getting dark and I was heading back to my Piper when I heard shouts.

'Stop him – arrest him!'

I turned round and saw Flight Lieutenant Mach, the main political officer at the Pardubice advanced flying school, running towards me.

'You're not allowed to fly!' he screamed into my face.

'Don't be stupid, I've got a flight order signed by General Rypl,' I protested and showed him my order.

'That makes no difference. I won't allow you to fly!' he insisted.

'If you say so. Let's go back to the office and let the General decide.'

I had no idea what was said on the phone but Mach stormed out of the office and barked, 'Go ahead, you can fly!'

On landing back in Hradec Kralove I taxied to the hangar as usual, but as soon as I got out of the cockpit, I was arrested by an armed guard and escorted to the commander's office. When the guard left, General Rypl proceeded to explain the events.

'My dear chap, the situation is very serious. Some ex-RAFs defected and until it's proven that you had nothing to do with it, you are under house arrest, but we haven't got a suitable cell for officers here.' He dismissed me when I promised to behave.

I used the time of my house arrest to study for my forthcoming entrance exam to the Military Academy. At the same time I filed for medical reassessment, just in case things got worse.

Ten days later I had a visit from the OBZ officer who escorted me to the commander's office where I was greeted like a long-lost son.

'I am so glad, all is sorted, you are in the clear and can carry on as before.' And he rubbed his together hands again.

I took advantage of his good mood and asked for two weeks' leave to organize my wedding. He agreed and I then gave him my application for a medical reassessment.

He gave it back to me, saying, 'My dear friend, I will not endorse it – you have got your whole career in front of you!'

On the way out I met his Adjutant, Flight Lieutenant Sebesta, gave him my application and told him to send it off the next day anyway.

The lectures and practical flying were in full swing and time went by very quickly. Before I knew it, my wedding day arrived. I borrowed a car from a family friend and, together with my bride-to-be, her mother and grandpa, we travelled to Moravia where we stayed in a hotel in the town of Kromeriz.

On the morning of our wedding, 25 June 1949, we picked up my best man – my oldest brother – and drove to the Velehrad basilique. The ceremony was only for close family members and after exchanging our vows we had a wedding breakfast in my birthplace of Lutopecny near Kromeriz. After the traditional Moravian wedding feast we returned to Prague, keenly awaited by numerous friends who helped us consume boxes of home-made wedding cakes.

On my return to duty I learned that I had been given a flat – it only had one bedroom and was on the fifth floor of a block with no lift, but at least we had some privacy.

In July I was given another period of medical leave – again to Trencianske Teplice Spa. I took my new wife with me and we turned it into a four-week honeymoon – this time there were no arrests or other interruptions.

A surprise was awaiting my return – I was given yet another posting, this time as commander of the Auxiliary Flight of Air Force Group 2 at Ceske Budejovice in southern Bohemia. Our joy at having the new flat was short-lived – but such is any soldier's fate.

General Rypl told me before I left, 'This is only a temporary measure, my friend, just until things calm down. You are indispensable to us and you will be back here before you know it!'

At Ceske Budejovice the commander of the group was yet another ex-RAF member, Lieutenant Colonel Frantisek Weber. I also knew the commander of the training flight, Pilot Officer Kamaryt.

I had lodgings in town while my wife stayed in Prague and we only saw each other when we could. It was bearable but even that did not last long before the wheels of bureaucracy turned once again and I received another order from the Ministry which dismissed me on medical grounds with immediate effect. Though my wife was pleased to have me back home, I smelt a rat. I was right. On 1 February 1950 I was dismissed from the service without any rights to a military pension.

That Christmas they exiled the whole family from Prague to the small village of Dusniky nad Vltavou, in the district of Kralupy nad Vltavou, where my only permissible employment was on the local co-operative farm. Dusniky, a tiny village of only twenty-seven houses, was cut off without a bus or train service. I managed to build a car out of an old German wreck I found in a scrapyard and we used it to travel to work at the co-operative farm in Vsestudy. My wife was an auxiliary accounts clerk and I was doing an agricultural land survey.

The house we'd been moved into belonged to the Military Council, which had exercised its right to take over the property just before the local Communist Party claimed it as theirs. This did not go down very well with them and one 'good comrade' made it his special duty to inform on us continuously. His reports ranged from 'Siska prints clandestine leaflets and distributes them' to 'there is the sound of a generator from his house ... he must have an illegal transmitter'. These produced a variety of reactions from both the secret police and the military authorities. Our house stood alone so it was easy for the police to patrol around it from midnight until morning for days on end. As our dog barked at them incessantly, we thought at first that they were burglars. The military were not far behind, erecting a listening device hut in a nearby hop field, and for three consecutive days a plane circled over the house. I had all the reports of their activities first hand – the local council chairman was an alcoholic and he knew he could get a drink in our house.

Into all this came the birth of our daughter Dagmar, the only blot on the otherwise happy occasion being the lack of a washing machine. The first twin tubs had started to appear on the market, but we did not stand a chance to get one as we had no money or the right to buy one either. So I decided I would build one myself. The basis was a wooden box and a small metal tub, which I had manufactured by some local craftsmen. With the help of a local blacksmith in the next village we melted some discarded aluminium car pistons and manufactured a small airscrew. As a former turner I made the rest of the parts. I only had to buy an electrical motor and a hand wringer, and we had a washing machine! I kept all receipts for the parts I'd purchased.

One day I came home from work and found my wife in distress. 'We had a visit from the secret police and they wanted to take the washing machine away,' she informed me tearfully. 'They want you to go to their office in Kralupy tomorrow.'

I took all the receipts and went to their office where I was accosted by two young men.

'Where did you get that washing machine from?' one of them asked.

'I made it myself,' I replied and proceeded to document the manufacturing process with the receipts.

'Where did you get the aluminium from? That is a listed material.'

'I used old pistons from my car.'

'You should have handed them over as scrap metal.' The other one went on the offensive.

'But I bought them from a scrap merchant in the first place and it was up to me what I did with them – whether it was making them into scrambled eggs or using them as a necessary part for my washing machine. Show me a document which says that I am not allowed to make my own washing machine!'

'That's up to us to decide,' the older of the two said rather lamely.

They were unable to come to a decision, so we kept our home-built washing machine and it served us well for many years.

In 1953 a nationwide survey of all farms was announced after the authorities realized that individual farms could no longer cope as agricultural machinery was in severe decay and they were struggling badly. My wife and I were asked to carry out the survey of the state farms of Kralupy district. During our visits to all the farms in the area I looked at, assessed and numbered each item, while my wife catalogued them. We finished the work before the official deadline and received a small financial reward.

At the same time the farm head office appointed a new personnel manager. She certainly lived up to the old saying about a new broom ... As soon as she found out that the farm employed an ex-RAF pilot whose wife voiced her support for the Canadian ice hockey team instead of a Soviet one, she took it upon herself to deal with such undesirables as us – she sacked us both on the spot. She didn't even bother telling us to our faces. Under cover of darkness the director's driver arrived at our gate and informed us that we should not bother coming to work in the morning.

We had been through a fair bit by now, but this was the last straw.

I went to see the director in the morning and, with the personnel manager present, we engaged in a lengthy shouting match. The result was as I expected – as an ex-RAF pilot I was outnumbered against the Communist-orientated leadership and was told in no uncertain terms that given my background I was unemployable. My wife, at least, was allowed to continue as an auxiliary accounts clerk, but at a sub-office at Velvary. Her daily travel from our house to work was an ordeal – to be at the office by six in the morning she had to get up at half past three. So for the time being I became a full-time father.

My war-related wounds started worsening again so I applied for spa treatment. In order to be able to even submit an application, this had to be agreed and signed first by the local council, and after that by the district military council. While the local council was not a problem – the chairman still enjoyed a glass – I fared much worse at the military one. Major Bruza hated all ex-RAFs and did not approve my application. He took no notice of my serious war wounds and considered that, as far as he was concerned, I would take the place of a working-class citizen. I demanded my rights in a somewhat raised voice and unwisely told him that I would pursue the matter at a higher level. In the heat of the moment I forgot about the telephone. By the time I reached the area military council office in Prague, its head, Comrade General Tondl was expecting me, and merely endorsed Major Bruza's decision. When I tried to complain about the accusations against me, he declared that though untrue, they were justified because as ex-RAF I could not be trusted.

In March 1953, President Klement Gottwald died. The new president was Antonin Zapotocky and the Party was lead by Antonin Novotny. Neither of these two changes made any difference to the attitude towards us ex-RAFs.

In May the National Assembly approved a proposal of the central committee of the Communist Party to carry out an immediate currency devaluation, even though President Zapotocky had said the day before that it would not happen. The exchange rate was a ratio of one to five and, for large sums of money, one to fifty. It did not particularly hit us as it happened ten days before a monthly wage payout. However, our village party chairman had 300,000 stashed away, for which he received an official party telling off.

The director of the Vsestudy farm lived at a confiscated farmhouse in Dusniky. One Sunday he was watching football and the TV packed up. He rang the nearest repair shop, which was in Prague, some 50 kilometres away, only to be told that although they had an engineer available, there was no transport. As I had worked for him before as a relief driver, he asked me to fetch the engineer. They welcomed me with open arms at the Prague workshop and asked whether I could possibly take the engineer to some other impatient customers in my area; they would pay me the going rate. We made an agreement that I would drive the engineer around and at the same time learn the job myself.

I got stuck into it. I gradually acquired all the necessary manuals and instruments, and got on with the job. As a lot of faults tended to repeat themselves, I soon got the hang of it and eventually became a local TV repairman under the auspices of the Kralupy nad Vltavou council enterprise.

Nineteen fifty-four was election year. The pre-election period was always a busy one and it was no different in Dusniky – the smallest village of the Central Bohemian Region. The first on the scene were the representatives of the Narodni Fronta organization who, according to the rules of the election game, had to prepare the list of candidates to be approved by the local Communist Party committee. Or the other way round – it made no difference as we were talking about the same comrades. But as there were disagreements about some of the proposed names, our village was the last to hand over the approved list to the district council. Even in a village as insignificant as ours it wasn't easy to submit a list. It had to include two new candidates, both non-Party members and newly arrived in the village, described officially as Citizen A (an employee of the local state farm) and Citizen B (a disabled person who as an ex-RAF pilot had been sacked from the same farm).

A proper pre-election campaign should have had a lot of media coverage, although this was not necessary in our village where everybody knew everybody's business. The last meeting of the pre-election committee was particularly eventful. Perhaps out of guilty conscience, envy or pure ignorance, the local party chairman and two female members proceeded to discuss their differences of opinion under the windows of one of the two proposed controversial candidates.

'I would never have appointed him as a secretary for agriculture. Every time he walks across the village green, he whistles to himself that old pre-war song "I am a gypsy king". That shows you!'

The other woman didn't want to miss her chance.

'The other one is no better. There must be a good reason why he was sacked and why his family were exiled from Prague. He must be a reactionary. They say he prints things and distributes them around. Remember the comrade from the district office said that we should not trust him at all.'

Perhaps the present party chairman had something to say as well, but before he managed to open his mouth, the wife of one of the two said candidates leant out of the opened window.

'Thank you very much for your input. I will pass it on to both men.'

The exchange that followed was not really repeatable. However, the village bush telegraph did the job and the information about it reached not only the two prospective candidates, but also the area party secretary and the chairman of the local council. According to the village weather gauge – behaviour of the locals in the village shop – we were in for some stormy days.

On the third day I – Citizen B – was invited to meet the council chairman and the area party secretary who informed me that both the Narodni Fronta office and the party had unanimously approved my nomination as both a non-Party member and such a distinguished anti-fascist fighter. I thanked them for their words, but I pointed out that according to the election laws only the best could be elected. I could not possibly consider myself one of them, judging by the publicly known discussion of the two women and the party chairman.

'You mustn't believe idle talk. We both know you better,' they said, trying to convince me.

After some more persuasion I agreed to accept my nomination, but only if the two women apologized publicly. If they wouldn't then my doubts would be confirmed and I would not be able to stand.

On the day of the village meeting, my wife and I were busy decorating, so we arrived at the meeting room, attached to the local pub, a bit late. Judging by the heavy smoke filling the room and the empty beer glasses the meeting had been going on for some time. At the top table sat the area party secretary, the local council chairman, the local party chairman, the representative of the district council and members of the local council. The village people filled the rest of the room.

The district representative asked if anybody had any objections to the proposed list of names. If so, they should declare their objections now. The heads bowed at the top table; others looked around. Nobody said anything. The wife of my fellow candidate leant across the table.

'Your two names aren't on the list.'

The district representative appealed again. Nothing.

'I've just discovered that my name is no longer on the list,' I said from my position as Citizen B. 'Any explanation?'

The district representative looked around and asked for my name. He then turned to those next to him at the top table.

'What's going on here?'

The local council chairman stood up slowly and with his head bowed said, 'It's up to the area party secretary to explain.'

'Why me? Why not you?'

The officials grew nervous and started arguing amongst themselves. So I repeated what had happened so far, every detail. Citizen A's wife then described the conversation she had overheard. One of the two accused women started defending herself, claiming that, to the contrary, she was saying how good a model citizen I was and how I had always been helpful to others.

To add fuel to the fire, the local party chairman confirmed what was said that evening under the window. After that the meeting got out of hand though, perhaps, with the heated discussion we now had a real meeting. The district representative eventually got it under control and announced that Citizen B should be put back on the list of candidates. But that was against the election rules, according to which an individual could not propose a candidate – it had to be done through an organization. It did not matter that he was a district council representative.

The arguments were flying around – some for, some against – endlessly.

A tall man with a big moustache and a pipe in his hand stood up right under the shadeless ceiling light and faced the top table.

'I swear to God, if I were a party member, I would throw the lot of you out with my bare hands!' He spat on the floor and stormed out of the room.

Some were in a state of shock, some were warming up to the situation. A portly woman appeared and addressed the top table.

'You should be ashamed of yourselves, talking in such a way about a man who fought for your freedom and suffered so much while you did nothing. During the Prague Uprising of 1945 you hid in the cellar and after liberation you crawled out and took what you could. Now you sit here full of yourselves, doing well. And you won't even let others live in peace!'

The tension grew and the shouting started. The district representative regained control and asked only party members to stay behind for an emergency meeting. The non-members went through to the bar, where we could not hear their voices and did not even notice that their meeting was over.

Needless to say, neither of our two names reappeared on the voting paper ...

Life went on. One winter's day I was coming back from a visit to the dentist in Kralupy. At Kralupy-Lobecek, formerly an airfield but now part of the local rubber factory, stood a long queue of cars with a few people wandering around. I pulled up at the end of the queue and as soon as I got out of my car, a man came over to me.

'Comrade, I am taking you and your car.' When he realized my surprise, he explained. 'I need you and your car for some film shots we are taking here. Come with me to the office.'

I was told there that my 1936, home-built car was exactly the type and style they needed for filming a scene for a film called *Infidelity*. The fee was 100 crowns a day for the car and thirty for me. Much to the chagrin of the other car owners I was given a special permit and allowed to nip back home to tell the family what I was doing.

When I drove through the airfield gate half an hour later, I felt strange, back in my old environment. I was given a short brief and the film director gave me his own instructions. I had to drive the principal lady actress – Eva Klepacova, whose first major feature film this was – across the airfield to a waiting private plane. They

168

had to shoot the scene in full daylight, which was easier said than done at this time of year.

When it clouded over, we took a break and got some refreshments from the canteen near the main gate. As soon as the sun reappeared, they sounded a horn and we all legged it back. The direct route from the canteen to my position went past the half-open door of the hangar, full of small planes. We made our way past the door as a group, but the guard stopped me. 'Comrade, you can't go this way. You must go round the back of the hangar. Orders from the airfield commander.'

Perhaps my old leather airman's coat had given me away. That special feeling from being back on an airfield swiftly evaporated. I suppressed the immediate urge to leave the filming for easy money – the easiest way I have ever earned anything in my whole life. The filming took ten days ...

After ten years of living in our house, a local fruit farm manager bought it and we were given notice to leave with no alternative accommodation to move to. One thing, however, played into our hands. At the end of the 1950s a new law was passed dealing with property ownership. My wife owned, at least on paper, a small house in the Vrsovice part of Prague which she had inherited from her parents. It was occupied by a local butcher. I went to the local council there and asked, according to this new law, for the house to be vacated and handed back to its rightful owner. After a lengthy discussion the clerk said to me, 'Comrade, you might know about a new law but I have got the instructions to go with it and you don't qualify.'

'I will take this to court,' I said to end the argument and left.

On legal advice, I took the case to court which decided in my favour. But the party committee in Prague-Vrsovice wrote to us that it was not in the interest of the country and its citizens for the Siskas to move back into Prague.

We eventually managed to find a house in a village close to Prague and moved there in November 1960. The job situation wasn't so good, especially for my wife. There were no jobs going in the local co-operative farm but after six months she finally got a job as book-keeper at the paper mill in the next village, Vrane nad Vltavou. For the first year she had to walk to work through the woods. I was allowed to work for the local council as a TV repair engineer again and the rest of the time I busied myself in our large, newly acquired garden.

In 1963 I was summoned to the prosecutor's office at Pankrac. I could not help reminiscing in its long corridors about my time spent there under the Gestapo. The prosecutor asked me to relate my story about my arrest and imprisonment in Germany during the war – the stenographer was busy for an hour. When I finished, she wiped her eyes. 'That's an unbelievable story.' But it was true.

The prosecutor told me that this would be used as evidence in a court case being heard in East Germany against the former Nazi lawyer Dr Hans Globke. A month later a messenger from the Ministry of Justice brought me a summons from the East German court and asked me to come to their office next day.

There were several of us: Vilem Bufka, a pilot with 311 Squadron, Gustav Kopal, a gunner from the same squadron, five Jewish women, and myself. We were told that on 10 July we were going to East Berlin as principal witnesses. We would not be allowed to have our own passports but would travel on a joint permit, and we would be met at Berlin's main station.

But met we were not. In the growing darkness we stood helplessly outside the station. After a while three official Volha cars arrived, an armed man stepped out of the first one and in broken Czech asked us to get in. We set off. The streets were empty and according to the signs we were heading out of Berlin in the direction of Oranienburg. The uniformed man in the front seat watched us in silence. We were all asking ourselves why we were going towards Oranienburg, which had been a concentration camp during the war. And why the armed escort?

A long way out of town we stopped in front of a massive villa. When our escort rang the doorbell a huge Alsatian ran out barking and we could only go in after a blonde woman called the dog back. Inside we introduced ourselves and the lady caretaker explained to us that we were in a government villa in which Soviet Premier Khrushchev had stayed recently. The three of us ex-RAF's shared a three-bedroom apartment and were served a first-class dinner on silver by a waiter wearing a dinner jacket.

There was no shortage of coffee, cigars and even brandy. Back in the rooms we found baskets of tropical fruit, a real treat for us.

170

The next day we had a visit from three young lawyers with their secretaries. They were very pleasant and took down our details for the purpose of the hearing. On 12 July they drove us to the court building in Berlin. Official news reporters from twenty-three countries observed the court, and American and Dutch TV filmed it.

The hearing started at ten o'clock in the morning. I was called first.

Through the interpreter I described my experiences in the different POW camps and prisons I'd been through. It took me over an hour.

When I finished and returned to my colleagues our small group was immediately surrounded by reporters. The chairman of the Czechoslovak Committee of Fighters against Fascism, Josef Hlusek, embraced me.

'This is sensational! What a bombshell! You will all be rehabilitated!'

'I'll hold you to it!' I replied.

After giving evidence we were all made guests of the court for the duration. We airmen were taken back to our villa later that afternoon for a special dinner, after which we had a visitor from our embassy in Berlin who told us that an order had arrived under which we had to return to Prague immediately, guest of the court or not.

Despite this unexpected and hasty departure the three young lawyers and their secretaries came to the station to see us off.

My return didn't go unnoticed. It was Sunday and the day of the village summer fete. The village green was full of people when the black government chauffer-driven car brought me home, the driver carrying my suitcase.

The promised rehabilitation came, though it was not a full one and it came a year later. I was given the rank of lieutenant colonel (retired) and soon after was amongst the first to receive an Order of the Red Star ... I began to feel a change for better.

At the end of 1965 I was invited to see the Director of the Civil Aviation Authority, Mr Krebs. After a short welcome he came straight to the point, offering me the job as head of the Civil Aviation Technical, Fire and Rescue Service (TPZS) which covered all airports in the country. My task would be to visit all of them, carry out a thorough inspection of the current state of the service and submit a written report. If I took the job I would also be sent on a business trip to Zurich with a view to implementing their system in our airports. Mr Krebs wanted me to start as soon as possible, but there was a catch – this post was classified as 'special' and therefore fell under the jurisdiction of the Ministry of the Interior. When I heard this, I quipped that it was highly unlikely that I would be able to take the job as this particular Ministry and I did not see eye to eye. Mr Krebs assured me that he knew that and that there should not be a problem.

There wasn't and on the 1 March 1966 I started my job. My office was in a white-painted office block, known as the White House, just outside Prague Airport. I travelled from our home in Zvole in a Fiat 600D which I was able to purchase on the strength of being a holder of the Order of the Red Star. That's how things were done in those days.

I became an inspector of TPZS and had access to all areas of Czechoslovak airports. I answered only to the operations manager and the director of the SDL. In order to be able to fulfil my task properly I was lectured on all aspects of fire prevention as soon as it was feasible. I attended lectures at the Prague Fire Service HQ and studied the operational activity of the Prague Airport Fire Protection Unit. My knowledge of English served me well as I was able to study various sources, including the regular bulletins of ICAO. I began to gather any relevant photographic and other material about air crashes.

While visiting the airports I took with me the chief fire officer from Prague Airport – a fireman through and through. We started co-operating with local fire services near each airport and organized a series of 'chief fire officers' days' on all of them. After the lectures they would put into practice what they had learned – first just the drill without a real fire, followed by a full-blown exercise.

I obtained several old planes from Air Force HQ, which were due for scrap. We set up a situation with the plane inside a circle of sand to prevent the fuel spreading. Inside the plane was a dummy and everything was covered with several thousand litres of aircraft fuel. Once it was lit, a fireman wearing a special aluminium-asbestos protective suit had to rescue the dummy while under the constant spray of foam.

During one exercise without the fire, the driver of the fire engine almost hit the plane. Later he was so worried that he stopped too far from the burning plane so the foam could not reach. Perhaps this incident contributed to rejuvenating the fire brigades in which many older firemen, even retired ones, still served.

I enjoyed my job immensely. As before, I applied the principles from my little book by Marden, *Whatever you do, do it well*. It served me well as at the end of that year I was sent to Zurich where I was welcomed by the airport's director, who made sure that I had access everywhere. I took full advantage of this and came home with a lot of useful information as well as striking up new friendships.

My idyll after my trip to Zurich did not last long. In May 1968 I had a visit from two high-ranking officers with an order from the Minister of Defence, General Dzur, for my reactivation. Their reasoning was that I hadn't reached the official retirement age and therefore was still answerable to the Ministry of Defence. I could not argue with that.

Our department organized a farewell party for me at which I learned that had it not been for my sudden departure I would have got the award as the best employee of the year.

In June the Minister met a group of ten Czechs and ten Slovaks; I was one of them. We were selected as prospective candidates for a newly created rehabilitation commission of the Ministry of Defence. We were duly rehabilitated and I was promoted to the rank of Colonel. Some Slovak airmen who were found to have received an Iron Cross during the war were subsequently dismissed.

Each of us was assigned an assistant – a political officer with the rank of Lieutenant Colonel. We were not under any illusion that our work would be easy. I was in charge of all Czechoslovak airmen who had fought abroad during the war and was able to get several of them reinstated.

When the 'brotherly' help arrived on 21 August 1968, our life experience taught us that things would get worse and that we were entering another period of occupation. It also meant that us, the ex-RAFs would once more be forgotten.

A period of so-called normalization followed. All activity of our rehabilitation commission was stopped, its programme was taken over by the political wing of the Ministry of Defence and I was, yet again, dismissed from the Air Force in June 1970 – for alleged 'health reasons'. At that time there were Egyptian pilots training in our country, together with aircraft mechanics and other technical personnel. I found a job for a while as an interpreter.

By 1973 my health was failing. The wounds, imprisonment, post-war repressions and my new occupation all took their toll. I spent months in hospitals and had to undergo more operations. My worsening health made living in a house in the country, with a large garden, too much of a chore. We decided that we should try and find a smaller, more suitable house nearer Prague, if possible, and eventually succeeded in the spring of 1989 when another period of political thaw was on the horizon.

A year later I had my rank restored and the right to wear my uniform in public. In 1991 I received the Order of M.R. Stefanik from the hands of President Vaclav Havel.

Epilogue

This is the end of my father's story as he told it. But his life story didn't finish in 1991 – he carried on for another twelve years and died suddenly but peacefully in his sleep on Tuesday, 9 September 2003, only six months short of his ninetieth birthday. Despite his disabilities and failing health he remained active until the day he died. He was vice-chairman of the Czechoslovak ex-RAF Association 1939–1945 in the Czech Republic, and he was involved with the Royal Air Force Benevolent Fund. He also helped to raise a substantial amount of money towards the building of a Sue Ryder Home in Prague, in which places are guaranteed for the less well-off ex-RAFs and their widows. He gave numerous talks, unveiled memorials and helped to raise money for the traditional airman's ball. In 2002 he was asked to be Patron of 202 Tactical Fighter Squadron in Namest nad Oslavou, a front-line fighter squadron in the modern Czech Air Force.

When he died, he was given a full military funeral including a helicopter fly-past. His obituary appeared in *The Times* and the *Daily Telegraph* in Britain. On 28 October 2003, six weeks after his death, I escorted my mother to Prague Castle where, on the occasion of the Foundation Day of the Republic, she received from the President the Order of the White Lion, Third Category (Military Group) in memoriam – the highest military decoration in the Czech Republic.

So he was honoured, not only for his bravery during the war, but also for his undying effort to help others, to raise the profile of his fellow airmen and to make sure they will not be forgotten.

Dagmar Johnson-Siskova